An Introduction to Chinese Birth Year Symbols

Compiler: Wang Hongyin

The Tiger of Majesty and Power

Translator: Wang Hongtao

Global ePress, LLC
World Publishing Xi'an Corporation Limited

An Introduction to Chinese Birth Year Symbols:
The Tiger of Majesty and Power

First edition 2012

ISBN 978-1-936358-08-3
Printed in China

Table of Contents

Foreword

What do you know about China and Chinese culture? And how do you know?

Perhaps you know China and its culture by reading the Monkey King story in *Journey to the West*, a fantastic mythological novel by Wu Cheng'en (1500—1582). And if so, do you know the other animals in Chinese zodiac signs, or do you really want to know more about China and its great tradition?

You sure know that China is a great country with a long history and rich resources. Its folk culture is colorful and profound through ages to become a heritage, which is especially valuable in variety and feature. Part of this heritage, however, is *Sheng Xiao* (生肖), or Animal Zodiac Signs in Chinese tradition. And here we have compiled a set of books (in 12 volumes) about Chinese zodiac signs in vivid English language and colorful book design, to tell the story of 12 lucky and lovely animals in this regard.

Actually, zodiac signs are found not only in China, but also in other parts of the world. For human race starts from individual birth, and his or her time of birth is related to natural phenomena in one way or another, for example, to stars overhead or animals on the earth. And in Great Britain, to take only one example, animal signs are also found to be related to human birth as in China, but one of the differences lies in the particular animals involved in certain system to be meaningful to man. Perhaps, zodiac signs play different socio-cultural functions in different cultures and therefore, we say that zodiac signs are different in different human civilizations so far as we find and get familiar with. And so, an intercultural communication is perhaps necessary for them to become more aware of each other and, hopefully, better understood now than ever before. And reading is the cheapest and the most convenient way.

Zodiac signs in China is a system having undergone a long-term development through its early stage, probably beginning in Qin period (221BC), as a supplement to the *Gan-Zhi* (干支), or Stem-Branch counting system coming into being even earlier. It relates birth time (at any certain period in one day and night) of human beings to some animals, all together 12, real or imaginary, and their regular activities, to become a circle to amount to 60 years, a complete circle applicable to both man and nature. It was not until Han Dynasty (206BC—220AD) that the names of the 12 lucky animals and the sequence of their match with the 12 Earthly Branches were agreed upon. A sequence of correspondence between the Branches and the animal signs was thus laid down, viz. Zi-Rat, Chou-Ox, Yin-Tiger, Mao-Rabbit, Chen-Dragon, Si-Snake, Wu-Horse, Wei-Goat, Shen-Monkey, You-Rooster, Xu-Dog, and Hai-Pig in the order as such. Chinese people believe that the individual human life must have some similarities found in his or her personal character and fate to be shared with those in the behavioral habits and activities of certain animal, say monkey, of the year under which he or she happens to be born into this world. Even more interesting is the fact that, there is some correspondence between human activity as a whole, for instance, farming, worshipping, or festival celebration, on the one hand, and regular activities of this 12 lucky animals, on the other, of which dragon, the Chinese Loong, is a sheer imagination in Chinese culture. This is most likely to be the duality of zodiac signs that play their cultural functions in a human civilization.

This series of books, entitled *An Introduction to Chinese Birth Year Symbols*, is a joint product of modern writers and translators whose research and translation made a great contribution to the final English works in terms of English expressions with Chinese cultural contents to be signified, which is, after all, not native to the English language as a signifier. And each of these books contains mythology and legends, symbols and pictures, customs and festivals, literature and arts, including paintings and sculptures, coins and stamps, potteries and porcelains, and other forms of instructions and entertainments — each aspect bears some unique features and special values of its kind. Readable and informative, we hope, are this series now presented before you, dear English reader.

The whole set of these 12 books are based on similar choice and arrangement of the contents. First, an introduction to the Chinese zodiac culture as a whole, and then each of the 12 animals discussed in detail, and last, we have a list of important persons grouped according to their birth year, that is, according to the same animal they share by birth, provided with their life stories and for some, also their portraits. There are emperors and empresses, generals and intellectuals, painters and poets, etc. some of them are already mentioned or depicted in some length or discussed to some extent in the pages before. It is also provided, with quotations of prose or poetry together with human life stories and experiences, and usually, in the context of cultural theories and patterns whatsoever, to contribute to a deeper explanation of the Chinese culture as a whole. And its fundamental spirit, as we know about Chinese culture, is man and nature in one process of the world.

We hope that this set of books would be lucky enough to gain some popularity in the English spoken world around, with active cooperation of our readers and friends. And we also hope that peoples allover this world would live a peaceful and happy life through intercultural communication and mutual understanding in variety of ways, of which, reading, we believe, is the most cheap and convenient.

Wang Hongyin
Professor of Nankai University
Tianjin, P.R. China
Oct. 2011

月

Introduction

"There are twelve in total, and each person has one." China is the most populated country in the world, but ancient Chinese wisdom is good enough to divide all humanity into twelve categories in terms of the animal zodiac signs, so that each individual, however different from one another, knows where he or she should belong and where to find his or her companionship in this regard.

The Twelve Animal Zodiac Signs, Clay Figurine, Shaanxi Province

The Animal Zodiac Signs in China

Animal zodiac signs, known as *Sheng Xiao*（生肖）, or *Shu Xiang*（属相）in Chinese, is an indispensable part of Chinese culture, which enjoys a widespread belief among the populace. For each Chinese individual, from one's birth, he is unavoidably tied to this *Sheng Xiao*. For a start, the *Sheng Xiao* influences one's whole life, from the cradle to the grave, that is, from the birth rite through the puberty rite, during one's wedding to his funeral in the end. Besides, custom has it that one's personality resembles, in one way or another, the living habit and behavior and even the figure of the animal he belongs to, for the Chinese character "Xiao"（肖）means "to resemble or to be like". Seen from a wider perspective, the *Sheng Xiao* is in evidence in almost every aspect of Chinese culture, ranging from ancient mythology to local customs, from diversified socializing rituals to numerous historical resorts, and from voluminous literary works to amazing craftsmanship.

The twelve zodiac signs are made up of twelve lucky animals, namely: rat, ox, tiger, rabbit, dragon, snake, horse, sheep, monkey, rooster, dog and pig. Among them,

The Twelve Animal Zodiac Signs, Clay Figurine, Shaanxi Province

the dragon is the only fictional creature, the rest of them being "real" animals, which can be divided into three types. One is the completely-tamed livestock: the ox, the horse, the sheep, the rooster, the dog and the pig; the second is the half-tamed animals: the rabbit and the monkey; and the last type are those so wild that some people are afraid of or loathe to see them, namely: the tiger, the rat, and the snake. For a long time, people keep asking questions like "When did the animal zodiac signs become symbols of a human's birth year?" "How did the animal zodiac signs come into being?" "Why are these twelve animals lucky, not the others?" and "What is the ordering principle of them?" Such questions remain yet to be answered. Of course, various attempts at a solution have been made through the ages. Some dig into the folklore and leave us a rich legacy of myths and legends. Some endeavor to relate religion to folk culture, only adding a more mysterious touch to legendary stories. And the rest undertake serious research,based on documented literature and unearthed cultural relics, in the hope of offering a rational solution to the questions above. Even today, these questions of origin remain a riddle, as does the Sphinx riddle in the West. And this Chinese Sphinx-like riddle, perhaps, could be solved some day in the future.

Origin of the Animal Zodiac Signs

Animal zodiac signs first appeared in the Chinese classical works before the Qin Dynasty (221BC), as a supplement to the *Gan-Zhi* (干支), or Stem-Branch counting system. The ten Heavenly Stems and twelve Earthly Branches were found in the oracle bones in the late Shang Dynasty (1600BC—1046BC). Later, the twelve animals

Bronze Mirror Engraved with the Twelve Animal Zodiac Signs

Bronze Mirror Engraved with the Four Deities and the Twelve Animal Zodiac Signs

Bronze Mirror Engraved with the Twelve Animal Zodiac Signs

Bronze Mirror Engraved with the Twelve Animal Zodiac Signs

Bronze Drum Carved with the Twelve Animal Zodiac Signs, Guangxi Autonomous Region

Circlet Engraved with the Twelve Animal Zodiac Signs, Guizhou Province

Bracelets Engraved with the Twelve Animal Zodiac Signs, Guizhou Province

Bronze Mirror Engraved with the Twelve Animal Zodiac Signs

Double–Happiness Animal Signs, Paper Cut, Shandong Province

The Twelve Animal Zodiac Signs, Clay Figurine, Shaanxi Province

were used as symbols for the twelve branches. In the Lesser Odes part of *the Book of Songs*, a poem "*Auspicious Day*" reads, "Geng-Wu is the auspicious day for me to hunt on horseback". Geng-Wu, a combination of the Stem and the Branch, was used to reckon the day and the Branch Wu was related to the horse. In the "Yue Ling" Chapter of *the Book of Rites*, it reads, "In the third month of the winter…the ox is seen". Certain relation was built up between the branch Chou and the ox to record the month. Later, a direct match between the twelve animal symbols and the twelve Earthly Branches

The Twelve Animal Zodiac Signs, Dough Figurine, Shanxi Province

Quilt Patterned with the Twelve Animal Zodiac Signs, Shanxi Province

Bellyband Embroidered with the Twelve Animal Zodiac Signs, Embroidery

The Twelve Animal Zodiac Signs, Paper Cut, Liaoning Province

The Twelve Animal Zodiac Signs, The Republic of China, Shandong Province

was established to count the day. In 1975, the bamboo *Solar Book A* of Qin Dynasty was unearthed in Yunmeng Shuihudi in Hubei Province.The Thief section records certain relations between the day of an offense and the animal. A resultant branch-animal match was established. Meanwhile,in 1986, another *Solar Book A* was unearthed in Fangmatan of Tianshui,Gansu Province which also records a branch-animal match with a slight variation. Obviously the two matching patterns belong to the Chu culture in the South and the Qin culture in the North respectively and the difference in the sequencing and naming process of the signs reflects an immature formation stage of the

The Twelve Animal Zodiac Signs, Weifang New Year Picture

animal zodiac signs at that time.

It was not until in the Han Dynasty (206BC—220AD) that the names of the twelve lucky animals and the sequence of their match with the twelve Earthly Branches were agreed on. Evidences can be found in Wang Chong's book *Discourses Weighed in the Balance* and Cai Yong's book *Questions and Answers about Yue Ling*. The chapter of "Momentum" in *Discourses Weighed in the Balance* records that "Yin (one of the twelve Branches), is related to wood and its animal sign is the tiger. Xu is related to earth and its animal sign is the dog. Chou and Wei are both related to earth and their animal signs are the ox and the goat respectively... Hai and Zi are related to water and their animal signs are the pig and the rat correspondingly. Si and Wu are related to fire and their animal signs are the snake and the horse. The animal signs of You, Mao and Shen are the rooster, the rabbit and the monkey, respectively." In *About Poison*, he supplemented, "the Branches Chen and Si are located in the Southeast and their animal signs are the dragon and the snake correspondingly", a notion which is in accordance with the *yin* and *yang* (阴阳) and the

The Pattern of the Bronze Mirror Engraved with the Twelve Animal Zodiac Signs, the South Dynasty

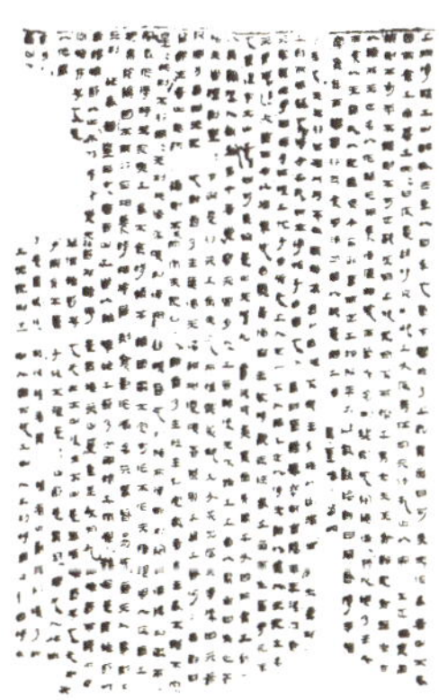

Silk Book, Western Han Dynasty, Hunan Province

The Twelve Animal Zodiac Signs with Human Body, Paper Cut, Shandong Province

Terracotta Figurines of the Twelve Animal Zodiac Signs, Tang Dynasty, Shaanxi Province

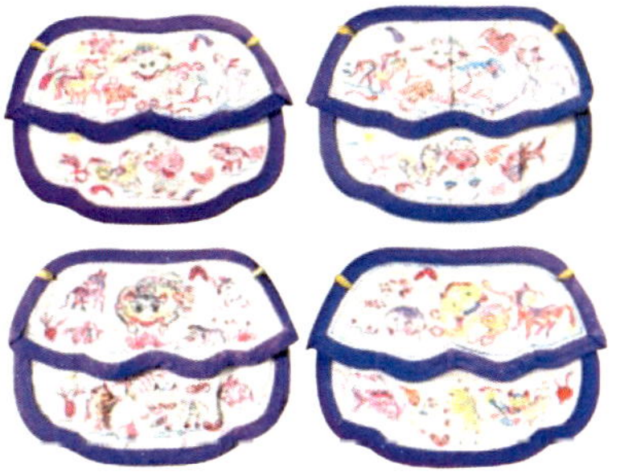

Pouch Embroidered with Children and Animals, Embroidery

Pastry Mould in Form of the Twelve Animal Zodiac Signs, Modern, Shandong Province

Five Elements (五行) theory in general. A sequence of correspondence between the Branches and the animal signs was therefore laid down in the order as such, i.e. Zi-Rat, Chou-Ox, Yin-Tiger, Mao-Rabbit, Chen-Dragon, Si-Snake, Wu-Horse, Wei-Sheep, Shen-Monkey, You-Rooster, Xu-Dog, and Hai-Pig.

The twelve pairs did not, however, find themselves in the orthodox classics as the way of recording the year; after all, a 12-year cycle is far shorter than a 60-year cycle which came earlier and was based on the Stem-Branch system. That explains why the animal zodiac signs, even though much the same as the Stem-Branch system to some extent, could not take the place of the latter when it comes to chronological record of historical events. Actually, the animal zodiac signs were adopted by some minority ethnic authorities as the official sequence of recording the year. The Tibetan calendar, for instance, is a variation of the Stem-Branch system. Legend has it that the Tibetan calendar had something to do with Princess Wencheng of the Tang Dynasty (641AD). It uses the Five Elements to represent the ten Heavenly Stems,

The Twelve Animal Zodiac Signs with the Shape of Human, Paper Cut, Shanxi Province

and the twelve animal signs to represent the twelve Earthly Branches. Therefore, the two Stems of Ja and Yi are represented by Wood, Bing and Ding by Fire, Wu and Ji by Earth, Geng and Xin by Metal, and Ren and Gui are represented by Water. So the Year of Ja Zi in the traditional Chinese calendar corresponds to the Year of Wood-Rat in the Tibetan calendar, the Year of Yi Chou to the Year of Wood-Ox, the Year of Bing Yin to Fire-Tiger, and the rest can be done in the same manner. A cycle in the Tibetan calendar is 60 years, or "Huideng" in the Tibetan language, the same as the Chinese Stem-Branch calendar. The ten-month calendar for the Yi nationality uses the twelve animal zodiac signs in the order of the tiger, the rabbit, the dragon, the snake, the

Wooden Block Carved with the Twelve Animal Zodiac Signs, the Republic of China

The Twelve Animal Zodiac Signs and the Twelve *Shichen*

The Twelve Animal Zodiac Signs in Colors, Paper Cut, Hebei Province

The Twelve Animal Zodiac Signs in Colors, Paper Cut, Hebei Province

Wish-to-bear-a-son Tablet Carved with the Twelve Animal Zodiac Signs, Tibet

Months in the Twelve Animal Zodiac Signs, Classic of the Yi Nationality

horse, the sheep, the monkey, the rooster, the dog, the pig, the rat and the ox. Because the tiger is the most worshipped by the Yi nationality, it comes first in the sequence. Other ethnic groups like the Hui Hu people, the Mongols, and the Manchu people in Northern China also borrowed the animal zodiac signs to record the year. *The New History of Tang Dynasty: Hui Hu* documents that "Xiagasi, the ancient country of Jiankun, records the year by twelve animals. If the year is of the Heavenly Stem of Yin, it is designated as the Year of Tiger". It was also recorded that there were two gigantic stone tablets on the top of Tai Mountain, one erected in the Year of Rat of the Taiding Reign, the other in the Year of Monkey (Gu Ningren, Archeological Notes in Shandong, as cited in Zhao Yi, *Gaiyu Miscellanea* in Qing Dynasty). Nevertheless, if decoupled with the concepts of the *yin* and *yang* and the Five Elements in philosophy or the reign titles in history, the animal zodiac signs alone as a chronological record of events are flawed in that they are not specific about the year.

Despite the inaccuracy in reckoning the year, the twelve animal signs coupled with the twelve Earthly Branches can specify a person's birth year without any question. As we know, few ancient people lived a long life, just as stated in the old

The Twelve Animal Zodiac Signs in Peach Form, Paper Cut, Shandong Province

saying, "A life span of three and half scores of years is few and far between." So the animal zodiac signs are used to record a person's birth year and can easily calculate his age. It was at least by the time of the South and North Dynasties (420AD—581AD) when the animal zodiac signs were first used to record people's birth year. In the book of *History of Zhou Dynasty: Biography of Jindanggong Hu*, it notes that the mother of Yuwen Hu, prime minister of the Northern Zhou regime, was put under house arrest by the Northern Qi Sovereignty. A letter was written to Yuwen Hu in the name of his mother under the decree of the emperor of the Northern Qi, which read, "when you were parted from me, you were just a little boy. I would rather not dwell on those chores. I remember you and your brothers were all born in the city of Wuchuan. The eldest was born in the Year of Rat, the second, in the Year of Rabbit and you, in the Year of Snake." This is the first record of animal signs being used to express people's birth year by the orthodox record of history. In its wake the correspondence between animal signs and people's birth year went down into many historical records. The book of *History of Southern Qi: the Five Elements* records a children's song about four warlords fighting one another: *"Though the wild boar growls, the horse has been evacuated from the neighborhood. Where are the dragon and the tiger? Wandering in the abandoned village of Jiangnan they are."* The song was followed by notes explaining that Prince Donghunhou was born in the Year of Boar, Prince Liang was, in the Year of Dragon, Xiao Yingzhou, in the Year of Tiger and it was not clear who "the horse" referred to. A poet called Shen Jiong between the Liang and the Chen Dynasties (520AD—589AD) composed a longer poem entitled "*The*

Constellation Chart with the Twelve Animal Zodiac Signs, Song Dynasty

Paper-cut Flower of the Twelve Animal Zodiac Signs, Shanxi Province

Fish-formed Basin of the Twelve Animal Zodiac Signs, Silverware, Guizhou Province

Auspicious Animal Signs, Paper Cut, Shaanxi Province

Twelve Animal Zodiac Signs" which read, *"Rats run over the dusty table; cows and sheep return to the fold at nightfall. Tigers' growl echoes in the empty valley; rabbits in the moon are seen through the window. Dragon marsh lies verdant far into the distance; snake-like willows wave in the vicinity. Malan*[1] *is now supposed to be harvested; Yangfu*[2] *is expected to be planted in the spring . Monkey corns taste better than fragrant fruit, and chicken (rooster) feet come as the best dish going with wine. Dogs miss their home, and pigs have nothing to do but eat."*

What, then, is the origin of the animal zodiac signs? Two theories stand out from amidst various propositions. According to Wang Hongqi's book *Mystery of Sheng Xiao Culture and Games* (Joint Publishing,1992), it takes twelve years for Jupiter to revolve round the Earth, causing the cyclical change of the plants in the Earth which in turn brings about cyclical change of the animals. The year that is propitious for certain species of animal is named after that animal. It is believed that a person born under the year of that animal will take on its characteristics and that animal becomes his *Sheng Xiao*.

Another theory, the totem theory, gains more popularity today. In primitive society, people tried every means to secure food and other resources from the potent and unfathomable nature, which they confronted with awe and worship. As a consequence, primitive religion and sorcery came into being, bringing about beliefs

1. Malan, also "malantou", a kind of plant. The first character "ma" pronounces the same as the "ma" of "horse".
2. Yangfu, also "yangfulai", a kind of plant. The first character "yang" pronounces the same as the "yang" of "goat".

Silver Ornament of the Twelve Animal Zodiac Signs, the Republic of China, Guizhou Province

in the harmony between nature and man, and the harmony between animal and human, since they believed everything in cosmos was alive with a spirit. Primitive people, much influenced by this belief, resorted to sorcery as the medium to solicit protection of supernatural beings, hence the nature worship, astrolatry, and animal cults developed. And then they expressed their worship for a certain animal, or plant, or any natural phenomenon by drawing a picture of it, or totem as is called presently, to be held as the guardian and symbol of their clan. In the book *Records of the Historian: Biographies of the Five Emperors*, it writes, "having the bear, brown bear, *pi*, *xiu*, *chu* and tiger (all are beasts of prey, real or fictional) in his command, Emperor Huang Di waged a war against Emperor Yan Di in the fields of Banquan." Each animal here represents the totem for one of the six tribes. History has it that the Xia tribe held the bear or fish as their totem, the Shang tribe had the swallow as their totem, and the Zhou tribe had the dragon, bird, tortoise, dog, and tiger as their totems in turn. The Quan Rong and Bei Di minorities in the North had the dog or wolf as their totem. Totemism can be seen in nationalities in the Southwest of China even today. The tiger, leopard, snake, monkey, and pig, for example, are the totems for the Naxi nationality; the tiger, bear, sheep, snake, rat and bamboo are the totems for the Lisu nationality; and the tiger, gourd, dragon, snake, rat and monkey are the totem for the Yi nationality.

The twelve animals in the zodiac signs are all pretty familiar to us, except for the dragon. Chances are these twelve signs stemmed from the various totems and after a long period of time took shape as such. They were originally used together to record the day and the month as well. In a silk book unearthed in a Chu Tomb of the Warring States period (770BC—256BC) in Changsha of Hunan Province, the twelve months in a year were related to twelve animals. Dongfang Shuo of Han Dynasty wrote in his book *Divination*: "There are eight days after the Festival: the rooster day, the dog day, the pig day, the sheep day, the ox day, the horse day, the human day, and finally the grain day. When it is sunny, the animals it governs will prosper; when it is cloudy, they will suffer from disease." The Yi nationality has the twelve-animal calendar which records the day by the twelve animals. Therefore, if today is rat day, tomorrow would be ox day, and so on. Three cycles, or 36 days, make a month, and ten months make a year. The animal calendar is not only found in China; it is found also in India, Egypt and Babylon. During the South and North Dynasties, the nomads in Northern China adopted it as a way to record the year. It is probably at that time that the Han people in China proper borrowed this animal calendar and then worked out the twelve animal zodiac signs by shaping the two systems of the twelve Earthly

← Legendary Emperor Huang Di, Ming Dynasty

Branches and the twelve animals into one pattern to calculate a person's birth year.

Naming and Sequencing of the Animal Zodiac Signs

How were the twelve lucky animals selected? And in what order were they arranged? Documents only tell us that the twelve animals correspond to the twelve Earthly Branches. As for why and when the correspondence was established, they offer no substantial evidence other than conjectures which mainly fall into four classifications as follows:

For the first conjecture, legend has it that Emperor Xuanyuan (Emperor Huang Di) needed twelve animals for his court escort. The cat asked for a favor from the rat to apply for him, but the rat was so bent on his own business as to be totally oblivious of the cat's request, thus causing longstanding enmity between the two species. The elephant also hurried for the contest, but was scared away by the rat who tried to get into the elephant's nose. The ox was chosen as the head, but the rat jumped on top of the ox to be the head. The pig, who caused confusion by saying that the rat was bigger than the elephant, was demoted to the last position as a punishment. The process went on and on, but anyway, through fierce contest, fair and foul, the Emperor finally selected the twelve animals in the sequence of Zi-Rat, Chou-Ox, Yin-Tiger, Mao-Rabbit, Chen-Dragon, Si-Snake, Wu-Horse, Wei-Sheep, Shen-Monkey, You-Rooster, Xu-Dog, and Hai-Pig.

According to the second conjecture, however, the twelve animals correspond to the twelve Shichen (two-hour blocks of time). In the Han Dynasty, the twelve Earthly Branches were already used to record the hours, each Branch standing for

The Twelve Animal Zodiac Signs, Paper Cut, Jiangsu Province

Waistcoat Patterned with the Twelve Animal Zodiac Signs, Embroidery, Shandong Province

The Twelve Animal Zodiac Signs and the Five Poisonous Creatures, Embroidery, Gansu Province

two hours of the day. The story "The Rat Gnaws the Day Broken" suggests that at Zi time (from about 11:00pm to about 1:00am), the earth is formless and void, with only rats sneaking in and out. They gnaw open the darkness and the whole world begins to see the light of the day. When the day is broken, the ox succeeds to toil the land at the following Chou time (from about 1:00am to about 3:00am). Yin time (from about 3:00am to 5:00am) is believed to be the time of birth. However, birth engenders death, the biggest threat which comes from the tiger, as believed by ancient people. That is why Yin time goes with tiger. Mao time (from about 5:00am to about 7:00am) is the time of sunrise. The sun belongs to li gua (one of the Eight Diagrams derived from *Book of Changes*). The broken line in the middle of li gua is the symbol of the jade rabbit, a creature believed to represent the moon. So we have Mao and Rabbit going together. Chen time (from about 7:00am to 9:00am) has the same gua feature as the third lunar month does when dragons exercise their power to cause rain, so Chen goes with dragon. Si time has all the features of the fourth lunar month when spring comes and snakes wriggle out of winter hibernation. Furthermore, Si time (from about 9:00am to about 11:00am) is also the time when snakes return to their cave. At the time of Wu (from 11:00am to1:00pm), the yang, or the positive, is at its height, but punctuated by the yin, or the negative, just like the galloping horse with its four legs in alternation between high into the air and down onto the earth. So Wu time goes with the horse. Wei time (from about 1:00pm to about 3:00pm) is the best time for goats to graze and fatten, while at Shen time (from about 3:00pm to about 5:00pm), apes whine and monkeys jump up and down at dusk. At the time of You (from about 5:00pm to about 7:00pm) the moon begins to rise and roosters return to their roost. In the mean time, the moon belongs to water and corresponds to kan gua in the Eight Diagrams. The broken line, or the yinyao, in the middle of the gua suggests the morning

Paper-cut Vases of the Twelve Animal Zodiac Signs, Shaanxi Province "Vase", pronounces the same with the"ping" (means peaceful). The twelve vases in different shapes are simple but exquisite.

Pillar-top of the Twelve Animal Zodiac Signs, Bone Carving, Henan Province

Auspicious Animal Signs, Paper Cut, Shaanxi Province

rooster. At Xu time (from about 7:00pm to about 9:00pm) the night falls and dogs begin their night watch. At the time of Hai (from about 9:00pm to about 11:00pm) the world is all darkness, the same way as the muddle-headed pigs. The statements above could be found in Zhu Xi's works in the Song Dynasty and other sources in the Qing Dynasty.

The third assumption comes from the concept of the *yin* and *yang* and the Five Elements theory. Animals are divided into *yin* and *yang* categories according to the number of their toes. The odd-toed animals are assigned to the *yang*, whereas the even-toed animals to the *yin*. *Yin* and *yang* animals are arranged by turns. The rat, for example, has four toes in its fore legs, representing the *yin* of the midnight, and five toes in its hind legs, representing the *yang* of the day. So the rat represents exactly the turn of the day at Zi time. Moreover, the rat, being both even-toed in its fore legs and odd-toed in its hind legs, is rare to see, so it ranks the first. The even-toed ox comes next, its four toes representing the *yin*, and then the odd-toed tiger ranks the third with five toes representing the *yang*. The rarer case is the snake, which has no toe at all, and so equals to the even number, and belongs to the yin. So do the rest of the animals in the sequence according to the same principle formulated in a book about *Sheng Xiao* by Lang Ying in the Ming Dynasty.

The last theory as assumed correlates the twelve *Shichen* represented by the twelve Earthly Branches to the animals' activity pattern. At the time of Zi, the rat comes out looking for food, and the Chou time is the time of rumination for the ox. The tiger goes around hunting for its prey at Yin time, and the rabbit busies itself grinding the herb medicine at Mao time. The dragon exercises the power to cause rain at Chen time and the snake returns to the cave after feeding itself at Si time. At the time of Wu the horse is ready to set off and at the time of Wei the sheep grazes and fattens. The monkey jumps up and down at Shen time, the rooster returns to their roost at You time and the pig is already sound asleep at Hai time.

The four theories above are put forward in a hope of offering explanations in the

The Twelve Animal Zodiac Signs and Children, Wooden Block New Year Picture →

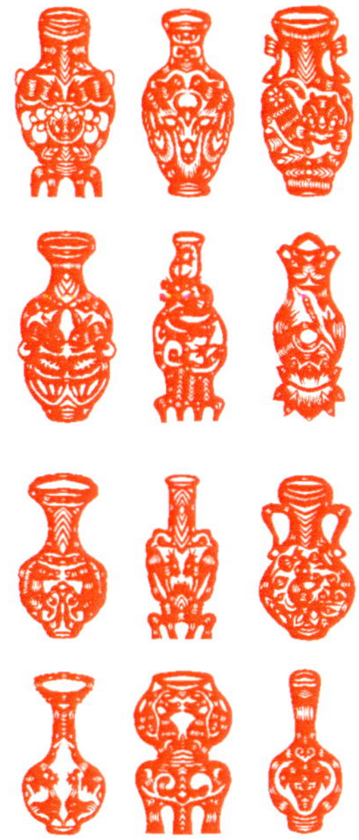

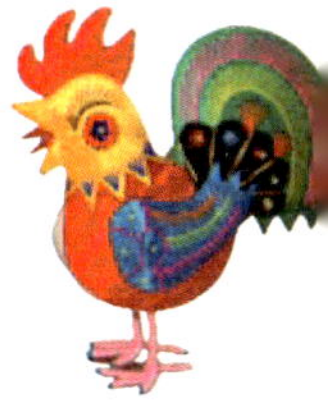

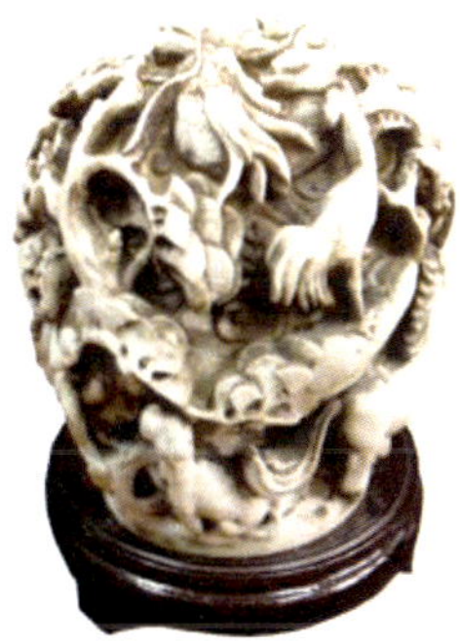

light of traditional Chinese knowledge of time, mainly based on keen observations of the animals' behavior in nature. In spite of legendary explanations, one thing is for sure, the naming and the sequencing of the twelve zodiac signs have undergone development through a long period in history. It is only with the growing knowledge of the workings in nature and the awareness of the activity pattern of the animals that people selected the best representative twelve animals as the traditional zodiac signs for humanities.

Suggestions for a new set of zodiac signs are recently found on the Web. Some people deem that the rat, snake, rooster and pig should be superseded by the lion, fish, phoenix and crane, on the ground that the rat steals crops and destroys furniture and clothes; the snake is vile and has a bad reputation; the rooster, or *ji* in Chinese *Pinyin*, is pronounced the same as the *ji* of "famine", indicating an ill omen; and finally the lazy and dirty pig is disgusting by all means. By replacing these four animals all zodiac signs would bear positive values as the lion is the king in the realm of beasts; the phoenix could be matched with the dragon in imagination and the combination of the two foretells prosperity; the crane is traditionally considered a symbol for longevity; and the fish, or yu, pronounces the same as the yu of "abundance" —all bearing positive values, though. While the new set of zodiac signs speaks more of the aesthetic inclination of modern values, the traditional zodiac signs are more deeply rooted in the origin and development of the Chinese tradition and are not subject to easy substitution.

Animal Zodiac Signs and Chinese Culture

As we know, the Chinese zodiac signs of the lucky animals manifest in a good variety of Chinese cultural forms. For one, the twelve animals are endowed with sundry personality traits. The rat is regarded smart and well-off; the ox, hardworking

and down to earth; the tiger, masculine and powerful; the rabbit, quiet and witty; the dragon, respectable and lofty; the snake, beguiling and mysterious; the horse, energetic and unbridled; the sheep, good-tempered and gentle; the monkey, clever and outgoing; the rooster, proud and auspicious; the dog, loyal and brave; and finally the pig, lazy but blessed.

Next, the Chinese zodiac signs find their way into myths and legendary stories. Actually, we have stories like "The Rat Gnaws the Day Broken", "The Rat Marries His Daughter", "The Cowherd and the Weaver Girl", "The Jade Rabbit Grinds the Herb Medicine", "The Dragon Shepherdess", "Madam White Snake and Scholar Xuxian", and "The Monkey King Rebels in the Heavenly Palace", to name but a few.

The Twelve Animal Zodiac Signs, Pendants, Shaanxi Province

Also the *Suishi*（岁时）, or festivals and customs, are closely related to the zodiac signs. The twenty-fourth day of the second lunar month, the lunar New Year's Eve and the fifteenth day of the first lunar month are the days of "Zhao Xu Hao", a custom of putting the lamp under the bed to drive away evils. The day of lichun, a solar term meaning the beginning of the spring, starts the practice of "Bian Chun Niu", whipping the cows to plough the land. In Guangdong province, people will offer sacrifices to the paper-made white tiger to get rid of bad luck. The Han nationality will hang up the head of the flour-made rabbit on the first day of the first lunar month, and celebrate the day of "Long Tai Tou", or the dragon lifting the head, on the second day of the second lunar month, and offer sacrifices to the Snake King on the twelfth day of the fourth lunar month, and celebrate the Day of the Horse on the sixth day of the first lunar month. The Bai nationality will offer sacrifices to the goat on the twenty-third day of the sixth lunar month. For the Beinan people of the Gaoshan ethnic group (living in Taiwan), every November after the harvest of the

The Twelve Animal Zodiac Signs, Clay Figurine, Shaanxi Province

Yansheng Coin (qian) with the Twelve Animal Zodiac Signs, Qing Dynasty, Shanxi Province

Bed Curtain Patterned with the Eight Diagrams and the Twelve Animal Zodiac Signs, Shaanxi Province

early season rice is the "monkey sacrifice" (puberty rite in effect), and the first day of the first lunar month is the Day of the Rooster. The Yao nationality will celebrate the Pan Wang Festival on the sixteenth day of the tenth lunar month, and the Zhuang people in their Guangxi Autonomous Region will celebrate the lunar New Year's Eve by hugging a pig and so on.

During one's lifetime in China, passing rituals and ceremonies go well with the animal zodiac signs. The Naxi nationality of Yunnan Province has the custom of sewing a monkey's tail on top of the newly-born baby's hat, symbolizing safety and good health. The Pumi people in Yunnan would drink beef bone soup for the puberty rite. On a wedding day, the Han nationality in Qinghai will entertain themselves with wine and some finger-guessing game. Whoever loses the game would go out to ride a horse and come back and drink again until they are totally drunk. At a funeral, the Naxi nationality will paint a white monkey on the front of the coffin, believing that the monkey would take the dead back to his ancestral home. Ancient people made yansheng qian, a coin not to be circulated in this world but to be held for afterlife use, with animal signs on it as mascot. They also made mirrors and household utensils adorned with animal signs. They wore a "longevity neck lock" graced with animal signs. From the cradle to the grave, their whole life was connected with animal signs. They were given names after corresponding animals at birth, and when dead, were buried with animal figures engraved on their gravestones and inside the chamber of the tomb in order to be blessed in this life and the afterlife.

As we know, China is rich in various ritual ceremonies. In Analects of Confucius, there is a story about Yanghuo sending a cooked roaster as a present to Confucius. Today, people of the Shui nationality in the South would entertain their distinguished guests by pinching the ear of a cooked pig, while the Miao people would present the heart of a chicken, the most cherished part, to their guests. The Kazak people in Xinjiang Autonomous Region would treat their distinguished guests to jemmy.

In addition, many places are named after such lucky animals. The Ma Wang

Picture of Apotheosis, Wooden Block Carving, Shandong Province

Blessed in Marriage, New Year Picture in Late Qing Dynasty

Picture of the Twelve Animal Zodiac Signs, New Year Picture in Late Qing Dynasty

Temple, Ma Shen Temple and Ma Zu Temple in old Beijing all bear the Character Ma, or horse, and in one place, the Ox is also used to name a temple. Such is also the case with the rooster, whose name can be heard on the outskirts of Nanjing City, by the bank of the Golden Sand River, deep in the Mountain of Dabieshan, and even a street, a city, and a county is named after this fowl, to name but a few examples.

Animal zodiac signs are also found in Chinese folk arts and one's daily life, such as on the paper-cutting designs, New Year pictures, colorful lanterns, and even on clothes. People also make stamps as well as toys in a set of the twelve animals and play games and sing ballads using terms related to the Sheng Xiao culture.

Animal zodiac signs find their ways into literary works. The Monkey King, the Pigsy and the Bull King in the *Journey to the West* are all animals, but they are also deities and human figures at the same time. So is the legendary figure of the Snake from the Ming novel concerning the Leifeng Tower by the West Lake in Hangzhou, one of the most beautiful places for tourism. Nor is poetry without animal zodiac signs. In addition, animal signs are also favorite subjects in ancient painting, sculpture, brick relief and carving.

All in all, deeply rooted in Chinese tradition, the Sheng Xiao culture has a rich connotation and a conceivable variety of forms in its application. Having a history of over 2,000 years, it bequeathed to the Chinese culture beautiful mythologies and legends, influencing and enriching Chinese people's daily life until today. It is really a wonder in the garden of human civilization.

Magnificent and Powerful Tiger

Cloth Tiger, Modern, Henan Province
A handicraft produced in west Henan Province, which is also nicknamed as a beauty of its kind because it is usually made with bright colours and delicate, lovely designs.

Among the twelve zodiac animals, the tiger is the most ferocious one. This large hunter of the Felidae family lived originally in the north part of Eurasia. As it migrated southwards, the animal eventually made its home to Asia, its last and permanent inhabitance.

The tiger is distinctive in its physical nature, which gives rise to numerous idioms, slangs and proverbs in the Chinese language with various connotations. The tiger has a big and round head. Therefore, "tiger-headed" in Chinese is often used to describe a robust and lovely child, while "in like a tiger, out like a snake" stands for anything with a good beginning but a poor ending. Tigers have strong bodies, so "tiger-shouldered" is taken to suggest the powerful build of a man. Inherently, this large feline has splendid colourful fur, as its whole body is covered with a tawny coat decorated with black stripes, while its mouth, belly and the inner part of its legs are dotted with white spots. That's why "the inherent literary pattern of the tiger" originally remarked in the Chinese classic *History of the Three Kingdoms* by Chen Shou is often used to suggest such a distinctive feature of the tiger by nature. Tigers are frighteningly ferocious, which brings forth such proverbs in the Chinese culture as "no one has the gut to ride on a tiger even if it is harnessed", "none dares to touch the moustache of the tiger", "as threatening as a tiger waggling its tail", "as frightening as a tiger dancing ferociously", "to glare fearfully like a tiger eyeing its prey", etc. In addition, "tiger-like nations" in the Chinese language symbolizes those that are aggressive and greedy, and the saying "a governor more fearsome than a tiger" originated from *Book of Rites*, which refers to a brutal tyranny. Far more interesting, based on the animal's domineering and solitary nature, the Chinese language comes up with such proverbs as "a fight between two tigers always ends up with one casualty", "two tigers can never live in

Ferocious Tigers in the Woods, Modern, Yangjiabu New Year Picture

Hunting in the Mountain, Painting, Yuan Dynasty The painting depicts the ferociousness of the tiger.

the same mountain", etc. In the same sense, "to sit on top of the mountain to watch tigers fight", derived from *Strategies of the Warring States*, a famous Chinese classic, means to watch in safety while others fight, then reap the spoils when both sides are exhausted.

Since it lives mainly in Asia, the tiger makes up an indispensable part of the Asian culture. In the eyes of the Asian people, both the physical feature and the natural propensity of the animal have rich signification. Its powerful build and colourful pattern aroused the mixed feelings of adoration and fear to the ancient Asians, which is well reflected in various nicknames given to the tiger. "Big animal" suggests the enormous size of the tiger, while "gormandizer", which was used to represent a tiger originally by the poet Wei Zhuang of the Tang Dynasty (618AD—907AD) in one of his poems, usually indicates the greedy appetite of the animal. Both "Mountain Lord" and "Mountain King" reveal the fact that the tiger is the ruler of the animal kingdom in the mountain, just as *Pian Ya*, an ancient Chinese hermeneutic book, defines it in one of its entries— "Mountain King refers to the tiger". Actually, villagers living in Northeast China respected the creature so much that they used to address the tiger as "Mountain God". Among the

The Tiger Descending the Mountain, Paper Cut, Shanxi Province

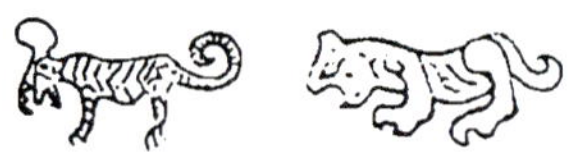

Tigers in bone and tortoise shell inscriptions and bronze inscriptions

The Tiger Descending the Mountain, Paper Cut, Shaanxi Province The tigers with their heads down and tails up share the same title, the artworks are usually put on the wall of the room as a protector of the house in China.

王

Twelve Earthly Branches designating time in China, "Yin"（寅）is specially chosen to match tigers, since the word "Yin" in the Chinese language means "respectable" or "awesome", which might be verified in such ancient Chinese dictionaries as *Er Ya* and *Zi Hui*. Therefore, to call the animal "Yin Hu"（寅虎）is to say "Respectable Tiger" or "Awesome Tiger" literally, revealing the respect of the Chinese people towards the tiger out of awe.

Symbol of Ferociousness

As a ferocious animal, the tiger is often taken to represent dangerous situations in Chinese culture, which finds expression in many Chinese classical works. *Guan Zi*, a famous book in political science by Guan Zhong (about 725BC—645BC), describes the tiger as "an animal living in the dense woods, which is so fearful to people that they record it in books". "*On the Fierce Tiger*", a poem by Xie Huilian of the Southern Dynasties (420AD—589AD), includes such lines as *"The fierce tiger lives in mountain woods; Its roar stirs strong winds around."* "*Ode to the Tiger*", another poem by Shang Lu of the Ming Dynasty (1368—1644), also glorifies the animal, saying *"The tiger is bold and strong; it rules over the animal kingdom around. As the tiger runs amuck everywhere, The whole kingdom is shaken by its awesome air."* Those vivid depictions reveal the ferociousness of the tiger in the animal realm, which is often associated with dangerous situations and is awesome to the people who ever see it.

Lots of idioms and proverbs indicating dangerous situations are based upon the symbolic ferociousness of the tiger in the Chinese language. "To pull a tooth from a tiger's mouth" means to take risks, while "to escape from a tiger's jaw" is to say to survive a disaster metaphorically. "One can never catch the tiger cubs without entering the tiger's lair" suggests that one could achieve nothing without venture, and "the tiger's lair" together with "the dragon's den" stands for dangerous places in the similar sense.

The Tiger in Fight with a Bull, Bronze Ornament, Western Han Dynasty, Yunnan Province

Three Hunters Catching a Tiger, Bronze Ornament, Warring States Period, Yunnan Province

The idiom "to tread on the tiger's tail or the ice in the spring", which originated from the famous Chinese classic *The Book of Documents*, implies that one is in great danger. Very often, "the forbidding strategic point like a tiger crouching or a dragon curling" is compared to the place difficult of access. In addition, the proverb "keeping the emperor company is like living with a tiger" advises those high-ranking officials to be cautious in order to avoid misfortune in their political career. Similarly, the proverb "to stroke the tiger's beard" is to warn one never to take the risk of offending those in power, as it was originally used in the Chinese classic *History of the Three Kingdoms*.

Symbol of Evil

Its ferociousness and greediness make the tiger a symbol of evil. According to Qu Yuan, a celebrated Chinese poet in the Warring States Period (475BC—221BC), the tiger together with the leopard guarded the passes on the way to the heaven, devouring the soul of people. That is why Qu Yuan wrote in his Poem "*Requiem*": *"My beloved King, your soul must not go to the heaven. Because the nine passes on your way to the heaven, are guarded by the tiger and the leopard, which devour the soul of those dead".*

The Tiger with a Bull on Its Back, Bronze Ornament, Western Han Dynasty, Yunnan Province

The Tiger with a Deer on Its Back, Bronze Ornament, Western Han Dynasty, Yunnan Province

Hence, the evil image of the tiger conceived by Qu Yuan has been quoted in many literary works including the poem "*The Journey in Snow*" by Wang Yan of the Song Dynasty (960—1279). Another story building up the wickedness of the tiger has been recorded in the "Autobiography of Song Jun", a chapter of the *Chronicles of the Later Han Dynasty*. As the newly promoted governor of the Province of Nine Rivers, Song Jun found that the local inhabitants suffered severely from both the corrupted officials and the ferocious tigers living along the rivers, among which, the former was believed to be the root of the pain of the people. Therefore, Song Jun dismissed the corruput officials and appointed those upright and able in such a vigorous and resolute manner that the tigers were also scared and "swam across the river, fleeing eastwards", which was also recorded and quoted in other literary works to take the tiger as a symbol of evil.

The evil symbol of the tiger could also be revealed in one of its nicknames—"Governor Feng", which was given from a story recorded in *Strange Tales* by Ren Fang of the Southern Dynasties (420AD—589AD). It was said that there was a governor in Xuancheng during Han Dynasty, whose surname was Feng. Transformed into a tiger suddenly after his death one day, Governor Feng began to prey on the local citizens. "Governor Feng!", shouted the people alarmedly as they recognized him. Hearing the name, the pretended animal fled and never returned. Seeing no difference between the two, the local people began to call the tiger as "Governor Feng" from then on since the dead governor, pretending to be a tiger, still brought disaster to the people as he used to do when he was alive. In the allusion to the story, Zhang Han of the Ming Dynasty (1368—1644) wrote a poem to rebukefully compare the corrupted officials in his time to the tiger, "The ancient governor of the Han Dynasty preyed on the local citizens, after he was transformed into a tiger following his death. The present governor, however, devours the people, when he is still in official robe and vigorously alive; The ancient tiger-governor ran away, when he was restrained. The present tiger-governor would roar to threaten, if he is held back. The ancient tiger crouched in grass; While the present tiger sits in court, devouring man and animal, as well as fish and shrimps". Moreover, the tiger was also compared to those ferocious and vicious people in other Chinese literary works including *The Five Poems of Asseration* by Du Fu, the famous poet of the Tang Dynasty (618AD—907AD).

Two Tigers Devouring a Deer, Bronze Ornament, Western Han Dynasty, Yunnan Province

Symbol of Gallantry

Hailed as a symbol of gallantry, the tiger is believed to be able to stir up great winds. *The Book of Changes*, a masterpiece of oriental philosophy, comments on the animal as, "the tiger goes with the wind, as the dragon is in line with the cloud". Annotating this concept, a scholar with the name of Kong Yingda believes that the tiger, as a dominating creature, and the wind, the vibrating air, belong to the same category of the nature, which accounts for the agreement between the two. Hence, the tiger is given the nickname "Wind Roarer".

To eulogize the gallantry of the tiger, Chu Guangxi, a poet in Tang Dynasty once composed a poem entitled "*Ode to the Tiger*", which includes such impressive lines as

"Its colorful fur shines in the morning sunlight, its teeth and jaw make it a great warrior. The clouds float as they are driven by its air, the ground quivers in echo to its roar..." A similar poem entitled "To the tiger" was written by Yu Ruyu of the Yuan Dynasty (1206—1368), which illustrates the courage of the animal by comparing it to an awesome general of the mountain whose roar at night frightens other animals into running.

The valiant image of the tiger could also be shown in many idioms. For example, "tiger's grandeur", "tiger's aura", "tiger's step" and "tiger's glare" reveal such gallantry as that of the tiger; "tigers howl with the rise of the wind" suggests that great men appear in response to the call of time thus could have great achievement; "to be born with a tiger's head and a sparrow's jaw" is to describe a man full of power and grandeur"; while "tiger-soldier", "tiger-man", "tiger-general" refer to brave warriors. In *Three Kingdoms*, a famous Chinese novel, the top five fierce warriors of the Kingdom of Shu (221AD—263AD) including Guan Yu, Zhang Fei, Zhao Yun, Ma Chao and Huang Zhong were granted the title of "Five Tiger Generals", while Xu Chu, the warrior of the Kingdom of Wei (220AD—265AD), who was valiant and stubborn, was hailed as the "Headstrong Tiger". In another famous Chinese novel, *Outlaws of the Marsh*, many of the heroes were also given the nickname of tigers. For example, Lei Heng was called the "winged tiger", Yan Shun the "silver-fur tiger", Wang Ying the "short-legged tiger", Chen Da the "jumping tiger", Gong Wang the "colourful-neck tiger", and Li Yun the "blue eyed tiger", etc. While in *Taking the Mountain of Weihu (Tiger) by Strategy*, a celebrated modern Beijing Opera, Yang Zirong, a brave PLA soldier, was also dressed in a waistcoat made of tiger skin to show his gallantry.

Silver Tiger, Warring States Period

Jade Tiger, Shang Dynasty

Gold Tigers, Warring States Period

Drum Hanging on the Bird-Bracket Supported by the Tiger-Pedestal, Warring States Period

Tiger Mask, Clay Sculpture

Tiger-shaped Hanger, Warring States Period

Phoenix-shaped Prop Supported by the Tiger-Pedestal, Warring States Period

Symbol of War, Penalty and Power

In the first place, the tiger is often taken as a symbol of military affairs, which might be best revealed in the ancient Chinese astrology. According to the astrologer, the seven constellations over the sky in the west, among the twenty eight in its total number, resemble the size of the tiger. The first one, which is called the "Kui Xiu"（奎宿）, takes the form of the tail of the tiger. The Chinese astrologers believe that if this constellation is bright, the nation would be governed by decent and able officials; otherwise, the nation would be ruled by a corrupted leader. All the four constellations including the second, the third, the fourth and the fifth, resemble the body of the tiger, with different constellations indicating different things. The second one is called "Lou Xiu"（娄宿）, the brightness and darkness of which indicate respectively the peace and war of the nation. The third constellation with the name of "Wei Xiu"（胃宿） is related to the livelihood of the people and the prosperity of the nation. The fourth is the "Ang Xiu"（昴宿）. It is said that peace is to come if this constellation shines bright, while slanders will spread among the people if it is dim. The fifth constellation is called "Bi Xiu"（毕宿）, which represents hunting and conquering. Constellation No. six with the name of "Zi Xiu"（觜宿） resembles the head and moustache of the tiger, the brightness of which is a sign of the well-being of the people, while the relocation of which foretells the subversion of the government or the discord in the court. The last constellation called "Shen Xiu"（参宿） looks like the foreleg of the tiger, the brightness of which foretells a good harvest. Since those seven constellations resembling the size of the tiger are in white, they are given the name "White Tiger", which is believed to be a symbol of military since it indicates fighting and killing. That the conference hall of military affairs in ancient China was called "white tiger hall" is a convincing instance in this regard.

Eaves Tile Moulded in the Shape of White Tiger, Han Dynasty

Brick Carved with the Picture of the Tiger, Western Han Dynasty

Brick Carved with the Picture of the Tiger, Western Han Dynasty

In ancient Chinese history, the military symbol of the tiger was used quite often in the army. As early as in the Warring States Period (475BC—221BC) in China, the copper tally issued by the central government to the local executive or general as the authorization for troop movement was given the name "tiger tally". The unearthed "tiger tally of Du", which had been used in the place of Du in the Qin Dynasty (221BC—206BC), was in the shape of a running tiger to represent a speedy army. Usually, the tent used by a general was called "tiger tent"; the flag held on the right wing of a marching army was hailed as "white tiger flag" to indicate that the army was as invincible as the tiger. Actually, the image of the tiger flag was so popular that it was employed in poems by such famous poets as Li Bai of the Tang Dynasty and Shao Yong of the Song Dynasty (960—1279). In the time of war, soldiers would hold "tiger-faced shields" to intimidate the enemy, and wear tiger-helmet to show their bravery. Similarly, various kinds of weapons they used including axe, crossbow, fire-arrow, cannon, etc. were also made in the shape of or with a design of the tiger; besides, many strategic passes, troop deployments and war tactics were named after the tiger, too. For example, one of the *Six Tactics*, a famous Chinese book about the art of war, is called the "Tiger Tactic", which was alluded by Yelü Chucai, a noted politician in the Yuan Dynasty (1206—1368), who glorified the

Bronze Tiger Tally, Western Han Dynasty

The Tiger Tally used by the Governor of Zhang Ye, Western Han Dynasty   Tiger Tally was something like a seal issued to generals by the Emperor as imperial authorization for troops movement in ancient China, which was usually made in two halves, with one being kept in the Court and the other being issued to the provincial governors or generals of the Empire.

Tiger Tally, Warring States Period

general of the army in his poems by the image of tiger. In addition, the image of the tiger also gives rise to many idioms including "dragons rising and tigers leaping", "fighting between a dragon and a tiger", etc.

Secondly, the tiger symbolizes the god who is in charge of the death penalty in the heaven. For example, "tiger prison" refers to prisons for those sentenced to death, and "tiger cutter" is a fodder chopper to execute criminals. According to the legend, with an axe in his hand which is used both as a weapon and the instrument of execution, the man-faced white tiger is the god of the fall, who is in charge of death penalty, since criminals are often executed in fall, which is also a season when crops are gathered and things would be terminated.

Last but not least, the image of the tiger stands for power in ancient China. When the officials were on their expedition tour, their guard of honour would hold a tiger flag and a tiger-headed tablet to warn against disorder. While in the law court, a fierce tiger was usually painted on the wall in the middle and the tiger-headed tablets were also displayed to create an atmosphere of stateliness. The bandits also took the tiger as a symbol of power, as the Chinese Opera *Taking the Mountain of Weihu (tiger) by Strategy* exemplified. In the opera, Zuo Shandiao, the ringleader, sat on the tiger skin in his chair to indicate his authority.

Symbol of Patron Saint

Being powerful and valiant, the tiger is also admired as the patron saint who protects people from the evil and disasters. The belief could date back to as early as the Eastern Han Dynasty (25AD—220AD), when Ying Shao, a scholar, collected and commented on the folk tales about the tiger in his *A General Introduction to Customs*, in

Story about White Tiger and Human Beings, Painting, Tang Dynasty

which the animal was depicted as a patron saint devouring devils. Actually, people at that time worshipped the tiger so much that they painted it on their doors and wore its paws as a protection. With the wide spread of the belief, the tiger being a symbol of patron saint found its way deep into the hearts of the people. In the temple, tiger was carved into the image on the bricks, stones, walls, and steles as the god of protection. In the household, the image of the tiger as a patron saint could be found everywhere in paper-cutting, sewing, toy-making and many other handicrafts. Specially, people believed in the magic power of the tiger as a protector of the children. So they made tiger-shaped shoes, caps, pillows, neckerchiefs, and even toys for young kids with the wish that they could grow up as strong as a tiger.

Symbol of Talent

Perhaps inspired by its colourful pattern on the body, people always take the tiger as a symbol of talent, which could be verified in various praises they sang for the animal. Li Bai, the famous poet of the Tang Dynasty glorified the animal by writing such lines as "the tiger roars in the valley, giving the rise of the wind", "those virtuous persons are as brilliant as the newly-grown fur of the tiger", to the effect that the talented people are

Tiger-head-shaped Neckerchiefs napkins made specially for children to catch saliva as well as a protector against evil spirits

A Tiger caught by Eight Hunters, Button-shaped Bronze Ornament, Western Han Dynasty, Yunnan Province

thus symbolized by the tiger. Du Fu, a contemporary poet of Li Bai, also eulogized the creature in his works by making an analogy between the talents of man and the aura of the tiger; more directly, Du, in a poem written for his great nephew, compared the young man to a roaring tiger, wishing that he could make great achievement in his career with the tiger as an example.

In addition, the tiger as a symbol of talent was also remarked in the Chinese calligraphy and the game of Go. In the art of calligraphy, "tiger-paw style" was used to name a special way of writing of the calligrapher; while "tiger-crouching", together with "dragon jumping" was taken to depict the elegance and forcefulness of the work of calligraphy. For example, Xiao Yan, Emperor Wudi of the Liang Dynasty (502AD—557AD), once commented the artistic feature of Wang Xizhi, one of the most brilliant calligraphers in Chinese history, as "his writing is as vigorous as a tiger crouching in the phoenix pavilion". Similarly, the tiger was also alluded to indicate the daring and incredible tactic a player employed in the game of Go. Liu Yuxi, a poet of the Tang Dynasty, wrote his poem "*Watching the Game of Go*", which said to the point that "the player is very bold in the game as if he has entered the tiger's lair, catching its cub; he is so skillful in the game that none is his match in the vast land of Hunan Province".

The Splendid Tiger Culture

An Animal Being Loved

Though the tiger is a ferocious and greedy animal, the clumsiness of its outlook and the simplicity of its character are lovely and funny. The positive side of it might be reflected in such proverbs as "as clumsy as a tiger catching crickets", "as fancy as the tiger to swallow the sun". Thanks to its positive image in the minds of the Chinese people, the tiger became a lovable animal in some of the legends recorded in various Chinese classical works.

The *Stories of Immortals*, collected by the historian with the name of Gan Bao of the East Jin Dynasty (317AD — 420AD), told a tale about the tiger as an affectionate predictor. It was said that there was a man called Heng Nong who was very dutiful to his step-mother. Woke up by a strange dream in which a tiger was biting his feet one night, Heng Nong awakened his wife and rushed to the courtyard. As they were kowtowing in the open air, the house collapsed, killing more than thirty people with the couple as the lucky survivors. *Tales from the Cheng Studio* by Lin Kun of the Yuan Dynasty (1206 — 1368) collected a similar story about a dutiful son spared by a kind-hearted tiger. According to the story, Yang Wei, a very dutiful son, went into the mountain to gather firewood together with his widowed mother. To their great surprise, they ran into a fierce tiger on the way back home. Yang, in tears, took his mother in his arms, and backed up step by step. Moved by the filial piety of the young man towards his mother, the tiger turned around and went away.

The Anthologies about the Tiger compiled by Wang Zhideng of the Tang Dynasty recorded a legend about a grateful tiger. Long ago, an old woman helped a tiger by pulling out an awn in its foot. Thereafter, the tiger was so thankful that it brought hunted hares and foxes as gifts to the old lady every day. What is dumbfounding is that one day it even carried a dead human body to its benefactress, for which the old lady was accused of murder and put into prison. It was only after she was proved innocent that she was set free. Taking it as a lesson, the old woman warned the tiger not to do this any longer.

Tiger and Butterfly, Paper Cut, Gansu Province

A Tigress and Her Cubs, Paper Cut, Shaanxi Province

Taiping Miscellany, one of the most famous Chinese fiction anthology compiled in the Song Dynasty (960 — 1279), collected a moving story about the marriage between a tiger and a young man. The protagonist of the story was a young

The Dutiful Son Lai Entertaining his Parents by Dancing like the Tiger, Yangjiabu New Year Picture The story depicted in the painting was traditionally known as one of the twenty-four filial exemplars in China.

Li Guang Shooting a Tiger on the Horseback, Wall Painting Brick, Gansu Province

Wu Song Fighting with a Tiger, Embroidery, Passed on from older generations

scholar called Shentu Cheng. Once on the way to his appointed post, Shentu went into a thatched cottage, in which lived an old couple and their young daughter. The young scholar was so attracted by the beauty and smartness of the girl that he decided to take her as his wife. Three days after the wedding, Shentu, together with his newly-married wife, proceeded on his way to take over the post. The young wife turned out to be a good housekeeper and gave birth to a son and a daughter, and therefore the marriage was a very happy one. When the official term expired, Shentu took his family and went home. One day, as they passed by the Jialing River, the wife, in great sorrow, composed a poem, saying, *"Though the love of a married life is true, the dream of a wild life is unforgettable. Once the time is up, the marriage can no longer last."* Hearing the poem, Shentu guessed that his wife was missing her parents. Therefore, they paid a visit to the old couple as soon as possible, only to find that the cottage was empty, which saddened the wife into tears. One day, however, Shentu's wife was so pleased when she spotted a tiger skin in the house. To the scholar's great surprise, she put on the skin without hesitation, changing into a tiger instantly, and ran out of the house and disappeared in the mountain. Together with his son and daughter, Shentu searched everywhere for her but in vain. Obviously, the tiger in the story proved to be an animal full of human-like love and affection.

An Animal Being Combated

As a possible threat to the safety of human life out of its cruel and ferocious nature, the tiger has always been combated by the people for the sake of their own existence. Actually, the Chinese ancestors had taken the animal as such a bitter enemy that anyone who could kill a tiger would be hailed as a hero. In the royal court, tiger hunting had always been a special recreation for the nobility to show off their valour.

Stories of combating the tiger have been collected

Wu Song Fighting with a Tiger, Taohuawu New Year Picture

An Jingsi Fighting with a Tiger, Zhuxianzhen Woodblock New Year Picture

An Jingsi Holding a Tiger Over the Head The woodcut was based on a legend about An Jingsi, a great warrior of the Five Dynasties, who once lifted up in the air the tiger he killed, with Emperor Li Keyong dumbfounded on the horseback

in many Chinese classical literary works. *Records of the Historian*, a masterpiece of the Chinese historiography, told a tiger-shooting story in the chapter "The Biography of Li Guang". Li Guang, with the nickname of Flying General, was a famous warrior and excellent archer in the Western Han Dynasty (202BC—9AD). It was said that

Butterfly Lantern

Sunflower Lantern

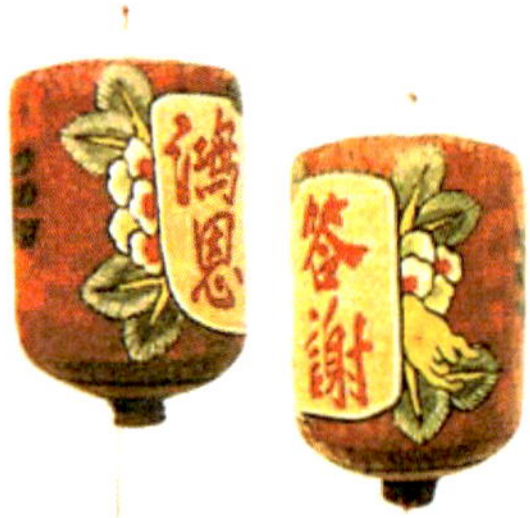

Votive Lantern

Mini Square Lantern

Three Fish Lantern

Lantern in the Design of a Fish Bearing a Tower on the Back

Golden Pheasant Lantern

General Li once shot a deadly arrow towards "a tiger" in the grass, which turned out to be a big stone. Though it was a mistake, the shooting was so deadly that it cut deep into the target. Another story of fighting with the tiger was tragic, which was recorded in *Xijing Miscellany*, a collection of legends complied by Ge Hong of the Jin Dynasty (265AD — 420AD). The protagonist of the story living in Donghai Province was called Mr. Huang, who had the magic to bring tigers and dragons under control. Once when he fought with a white tiger, Mr. Huang failed to give free play to his magic since he was old-aged and over-drunk. As a result, Huang was devoured by the tiger in the end. Nevertheless, Wu Song, a kungfu master living in the Song Dynasty, had successfully killed a tiger barehanded, as what was depicted in the *Outlaws of the Marsh*, one of the classical Chinese novels. Absurd was

Carp Lantern

Guessing Riddles A picture drawn by Zhou Muqiao depicting the excited spectators guessing riddles

Designing Lantern Riddles Unexpurgated Version of *A Dream of Red Mansions*

Riddles Written on the Pictures, Wuqiang New Year Picture, Hebei Province

a tale told in the *Legends* collected by Pei Xing of the Tang Dynasty. According to the tale, Ma Zheng, a scholar, once went to visit a certain monk, who was only found to have already transformed into a tiger. To Ma's irritation, his servant, who had been accompanying him, was eaten by the tiger. As for revenge, the scholar managed to kill the animal only to find that a dozen ghosts, who had grown out of those swallowed by the tiger, became its accomplices. Without any other choice, Ma killed another tiger, setting free those ghosts. Similar stories recorded in ancient Chinese works are countless, revealing people's resistance against this frightening animal.

Hanging Tiger, Clay Sculpture, Shaanxi Province A kind of sculpture usually in white or heavy colours, which is produced at Fengxiang of Shaanxi Province, to hang behind the door as a holy saint for longevity and reproductivity in the drainage area of the Weihe River

The hostile relationship of man with the tiger is also reflected in some customs, among which the celebration of the lantern festival is one. On the night of January 15 every year according to the lunar calendar, the most important recreation for the Chinese people is to watch lanterns, some of which are made in the shape of the tiger. According to the records collected in *Minghuang Miscellany* by Zheng Chuhui of the Tang Dynasty, a thirty-meter-high lantern tower decorated with tinkling trinkets would be built for the festival, on which people hanged colourful lanterns made in the shape of the tiger, dragon, phoenix, etc. While on each of the lanterns was written a riddle, which was also known as the so called "lantern tiger". Therefore, to guess the riddle was also called "striking the tiger" or "shooting the tiger", in order to show that to get the answer was as hard as to combat a tiger.

Tiger-shaped Pattern Design, Hubei Province

Another custom used to be popular in such places as the Yi County, and She county of Anhui Province, where people had the rites of "driving off white tigers" on February 2 each year of the lunar calendar. According to the local people, the white tiger was a demon haunting human beings in the early spring each year, so it must be driven off for the safety of mankind. The *Annals of the County Yi* explained the rites in details—on February 2 every year, people would honour the gods with delicious food including pig-foot first, and then they threw eggs onto the top of the wall, smashing them into foam so as to drive off the white tiger.

Tiger-shaped Pattern Design, Hubei Province

Though taking it as their enemy, people still worship the tiger as a powerful being, hoping, with the help of the tiger, man is able to defeat other tough enemies of the mankind. Therefore, in the mind of the Chinese people there is a mixed feeling of love and hatred, of awe and fear towards the tiger, which is manifested in various legends, customs in the Chinese culture.

An Animal Being Mystified

Tiger-shaped Pattern Design, Jiangxi Province

Although it is an animal living in the nature of the real world, the tiger has been mystified in various weird ways in the Chinese culture, as recorded in many Chinese classics.

In the *Book of Mountains and Seas* written as early as 2,000 years ago, some strange animals are described bearing striking similarities to the tiger, "There lives in the Manqu mountain an animal called Mafu, which has a man's face and a tiger's body. Crying like a baby, the animal eats human flesh." While in the chapter about the western frontier of the country in the book, another strange animal was also compared to the tiger, "On top of the Kunlun Mountain, which has a 100-meter-deep cliff on its southern side, there stands an animal with the name of Kaimingshou, which has nine heads, each with a human face and the enormous body was like that of a tiger". Obviously, both animals recorded in the *Book of Mountains and Seas* are based on the conception of mankind about the tiger out of fear.

What's more mysterious are the legends about the human being's transformation into the tiger, or vice versa. The story about "Governor Feng", as mentioned earlier, is such an example. Actually, the reason why the tiger was given the nickname of a man is that seeing no difference between the tiger and the corrupted officials such as Governor Feng, the people just called the animal ironically by the name of the wicked man to show their detestation to those malfeasants. Another example was recorded, in *More Stories of Immortals* written by Tao Qian of the East Jin Dynasty (317AD—420AD). The protagonist of the story was called Shen Zong, who made his living by fortune-telling. With lots of money in their hands, a man and his servant rode horses to visit him one day, asking for a suggestion whether they should go eastward or westward to find food. Shen told them that to go eastward was a better choice. To quench their thirst, they asked Shen for some water to drink. To his surprise, Shen found that the two men put their mouths into the jar to drink the water

Tiger Totem of the Yi People, Wall Painting

Gourd Painted with the Design of the Tiger Head, Artifact of the Yi People, Yunnan Province

as cattle did. What happened next was even more astonishing — both the servant and the horses changed into tigers soon after they started walking eastward for about fifty yards. From then on, tigers assaulted the neighborhood very often. *Taiping Miscellany*, one of the most famous Chinese fiction anthology compiled in the Song Dynasty, also recorded a weird story. It was said that the tiger, as it changed into a man, married a young lady, who knew nothing about it for as long as two years' time

White Tiger, Jiama Picture of the Tujia People, Yunnan Province

Tiger-head Mask of the Di Opera, Guizhou Province

Tiger-head Mask of the Yi People, Yunnan Province

after the wedding ceremony. Bringing wine with them, two guests came to visit the husband one day. Though she was warned by her husband not to peep as they were drinking, the wife could not help taking a look furtively, only to find that her husband, together with the visitors, gave themselves away by changing into tigers after they were drunken, though they turned into humans again thereafter. Greatly astounded, the wife managed to leave her tiger-husband in the end.

An Animal Being Worshiped

a.Tiger Being Worshiped as the Ancestor

Why could the tiger get married with human beings? The answer is that people from some minority groups in China believe that the tiger is their earliest ancestor. For instance, the Aketengka tribe of the Hezhe people hold such a belief that their primogenitor was the son of the couple of a Hezhe girl and a tiger. Stories about the marriage between human and the tiger could be found among such people as Bai, Lisu, Tujia etc., who live in Yunnan, a province of South China.

Yi people living in Yunnan Province, for example, call themselves a tiger race. Based on the complex about the animal, they coin many nicknames for both themselves and the tiger, for example, “Luopo” for a man or a male tiger, “Luoluomo” for a girl, “Luomo” for a female tiger, “Luozhi” or “Luoluo” for the people or the tiger in a general sense. What is more, Yi people also name lots of places as the tiger, which sound very much like “Luomo”. Actually, the tiger-worshiping tradition of the Yi people has already been recorded in many Chinese classics. The *Book of Mountains and Seas* wrote that an animal living in the North Sea looked like a tiger, which was called “Luoluo”, while *The Understanding of the Literary Expositor* by Fang Yizhi of the Ming Dynasty recorded that the people of Nan Zhao called the tiger “Boluo”, while the Barbarians named the animal “Luoluo”. Even at the present time, the people of Yi

Pictures of the White Tiger and Elephant as Auspicious Animals, Qing Dynasty, Fujian Province
Being the ruler of the animal kingdom, the tiger is regarded as an auspicious animal in China. According to *Pictures on Auspiciousness*, the white tiger, as King of the animals, is harmless and benevolent, with its kindness spreading far and wide to both men and plants. Therefore, many villagers choose the tiger as their patron saint.

living in such places as Liangshan and Ailaoshan still keep the cremation tradition simply out of the fear that they could not otherwise transform into tigers after death.

Being regarded as the ancestor, the tiger is worshiped through various customs by people from more than one ethnic minority in China. For the people of Yi, they record time according to the so-called "tiger calendar", which takes January as the month corresponding with "Yin"（寅） branch among the twelve earthly branches because it is in concord with the tiger that ranks the top among the twelve zodiac animals. In some areas, the Yi people celebrate the "tiger festival" from the dusk of January 8 to the dawn of January 15 according to the lunar calendar, wishing good health and bumper harvest for the next year. On the festival, people would hold such ceremonies as inviting the "tiger-god" in, dancing the "tiger dance", eating the "tiger meat", which is actually pork. While on January 15 , an old man, who is disguised as the mountain god or the avatar of the tiger, would pay a visit to each family to say happy new year to them since that day is believed to be the time for people "to see the tiger eastwards off ". For the people of Pumi, who also live in Yunnan Province, all the times that are associated with the animal such as the "tiger year", "tiger month", "tiger day", etc. are considered as lucky times, and the tiger ranks the first among the twelve zodiac animals in their minds. One of the most tiger-adoring ethnic minorities in Yunnan Province might be the Bai people, who not only call themselves the sons and daughters of tigers, but take the white tiger as such a holy god that they believe one could become an immortal if he or she is eaten by the animal. Very similar to the people of Yi, the Lisu people regard the black tiger as their god, and do not capture the tiger in hunting. As for the Naxi people, the tiger is a symbol of virtue and capacity, which has been recorded in details in "A History of the Tiger" as part of Dongbajing, the holy scripture about the history and culture of Naxi. The people of Naxi also regard the "tiger day" as lucky date which is believed to be the best time to

Crouching Tiger, Clay Sculpture, Shaanxi Province

Crouching Tiger, Clay Sculpture, Shaanxi Province

Colourful Steamed Bread made in the Shape of the Tiger, Shaanxi Province

Tiger as a Zodiac Animal, Clay Sculpture, Shaanxi Province

Colourful Tiger, Clay Sculpture, Shaanxi Province

make a trip or to give birth to a baby. Interesting enough, they even put up the picture of the tiger on their door along with that of the yak to wish safety for the family. In addition, many other minority groups including the Lahu people, Nu people, and the Qiang people of Sichuan and Gansu Province, Luoba people of Tibet also worship the tiger, as is revealed in their respective customs.

People that adore the tiger most are from the minority group called Tujia, who not only regard the animal as their ancestor, but also take the white tiger as their god. According to the archaeological discovery, Tujia people are the descendants of an ancient clan with the name of Ba, who originally lived in the region that is currently known as Changyang County of Hubei Province. In Changyang County, there goes a legend, saying that the local chieftain was called "Xiang Wang, the great son of the heaven". It was said that "Xiang Wang" was born at the Yin hour on the Yin day in the Yin month of the Yin Year, a time matching the tiger respectively. As the first ruler of the Ba Kingdom, Xiang Wang made great achievements in his reign. According to what was described in the *Chronicles of the Later Han Dynasty*, King "Xiang Wang" transformed into a white tiger after death, going back to the heaven ultimately. Sincerely believing in the story, the Ba people thus worshiped the white tiger as their god, which gave rise to lots of customs honoring the animal. Today, the people of Tujia inherit the tradition of their ancestors by kowtowing regularly before the cliff with the name of white tiger, and worshiping the tiger-god every day before its holy sculpture which has been put on the shrine of each family. In addition, people build

Black Tiger, the Divine Spirit, Shadow Puppet, Shaanxi Province

temples in many places along the Qingjiang River of Changyang County as well as in the Town of Xuan-en to worship the god of white tiger and its avatar "Xiang Wang". What is most unimaginable is that the people of Tujia adore the white-tiger-god so much that they even offer him human blood as sacrifice, which was also recorded in the *Chronicles of the Later Han Dynasty*. To observe the rite, the priest usually cuts himself on the head, shedding blood onto the joss paper, which would be hung up and then burnt so as to show piety to the tiger-god.

Actually, the adoration of the Tujia people towards the white-tiger god finds expression in many aspects of their daily life. Not only would people sing songs about the white tiger in their work of weeding, but also they would pray to the tiger

Tiger-shaped Copper Coins Strung Together, the Republic of China, Beijing

Tiger, Clay Sculpture, Modern, Beijing

god, asking for a suggestion about the proper time to get married. Even in funerals, the Tujia people would imitate the movements of the tiger in their dancing around the coffin, which must be covered by a tiger-skin-made blanket. Specially, little kids attending the funeral would wear a tiger-hat to save them from the scare of the evil spirits. Recently, a lot of unearthed cultural relics also show that the life of the ancient Tujia people was closely related to the tiger, as many musical instruments and articles for daily use that had been excavated were found decorated with the literary pattern of the animal. It is no wonder that the Ba Kingdom was also historically known as the "tiger land" and the inhabitants living on the land were called "the tiger people". In the same sense, the Ba people regard themselves as "a tiger race".

b. Tiger Being Consecrated

Though taken as a fierce or propitious animal, the tiger is consecrated in many places in China. In Guangdong Province, people offer sacrifice to the white tiger on either the 5th or 6th, or the 7th of March every year, which is known as the day of the "waking of insects", the third solar term among the 24 in the Chinese culture. Literally, the "waking of insects" symbolizes the time when various creatures hidden underground start to show themselves on the ground to search for food. It is said that the white tiger, like other animals, would also begin its hunting on that day, thus endangering human beings. For the sake of security, people choose to offer sacrifice to the animal on that day by feeding lard and eggs ceremonially to a white tiger statue, which is usually made extremely ugly and fearsome, believing that the tiger would no longer prey on humans so long as it is feasted.

In the provinces of Shaanxi and Shanxi, the tiger is consecrated in such a lovely way on the Chinese New Year's eve that people make steamed breads in the shape of tigers, which would be offered either as sacrifice to ancestors or gifts to friends and relatives. Those steamed breads are usually decorated with flour-made flowers or little animals, thus they are also called "flour flowers". The interesting decoration is out of the belief of the local people that the vitality of both the plant and the animal symbolizes the vigorous reproduction of their offspring. Actually, people living in the southern part of Shanxi Province offer to their ancestors steamed breads made in the shape of the tiger-head as sacrifice also on the Tomb-sweeping day (Qingming Festival) every year. According to

The Holy Tiger as a Protector of the House, Weifang New Year Picture, Shandong Province

Overawing the Animal Kingdom, Yangjiabu New Year Picture

Stone Tiger, Late Jin Dynasty

Tiger Guard, West Jin Dynasty

historical records, the inhabitants of such provinces as Jiangsu, Zhejiang would, on the day of Spring Festival, make the so-called "tiger-flower" to present to friends and relatives as gift, which is usually made of wool and cedar leaves in the shape of the tiger.

In the Hua County of Shaanxi Province, the animal is even taken as a blessing for the bride and groom on the wedding ceremony, which is best revealed in the custom called "hanging the tiger-bread". To observe the rite, the groom's uncle would make two steam-breads in the shape of the male tiger and female tiger respectively beforehand. The Chinese character "王" ("wang", means King) would be written on the forehead of the male tiger to indicate that the groom will be the head of the family, while two flying birds would be drawn on that of the female tiger to show that

Fighting with the Tiger, Rubbing of Brick Relief, Han Dynasty, Henan Province

Taming the Tiger, Rubbing of Stone Relief, Han Dynasty, Henan Province

Drama about the Tiger, Rubbing of Stone Relief, Han Dynasty, Henan Province

Fighting with the Tiger, Rubbing of Stone Relief, Han Dynasty, Sichuan Province

Stone Tiger, Western Han Dynasty, Shaanxi Province

Cloth Tiger, Shaanxi Province

A Flock of Tigers, Handicrafts, North China and Northwest China

Various Cloth Tigers

the bride is to accompany her husband in the future as a loyal partner. What is more, a tiger cub would be painted on the chest of the two grown-up tigers to signify that a baby of them will be born soon. On the wedding day, the two tiger-breads strung by a red thread would be hung around the neck of the bride just before she walks into the entrance for the ceremony. Soon after the bride gets in, the tiger-breads would be taken down from her neck and shared by the couple with the hope that they will give birth to a baby very soon, who, hopefully, would be as strong as a tiger.

In Taiwan Province, the tiger is also worshiped as god, but usually along with other deities such as Tudi god and Bosheng god. According to the legend, the Tudi god was the guardian of the local people, who had brought the fierce tiger under control as a request of the local inhabitants. Therefore, the tiger became the attendant of the Tudi god and was worshiped in the temple as the "Tiger God" ever since, who took the order of the Tudi god, punishing the evil and the criminals. While the Bosheng god, whose personal name was Wu Ben, used to work as a virtuous doctor in the Song Dynasty. Doctor Wu had once cured a tiger who was wounded in the throat as it swallowed a man it killed. Offering the medication, the doctor dissuaded the tiger from killing and made it his guard. Thanks to the redemption, Doctor Wu became the Bosheng god, while the tiger turned out to be his mount, hailed as the General Black-tiger by the people. That is why the tiger is consecrated together with the Tudi god and the Bosheng god in Taiwan. At the present time, the local inhabitants of Taiwan worship the tiger as god for two reasons. One is that the tiger is believed to be the god who could bring health and intelligence to children since it repels the evil spirits; the other is that the animal is also regarded as the god of fortune because people believe that the mouth of the tiger is so big that it could fetch gold and silver for them.

Cloth Tiger, Handicraft, Shaanxi Province

Cloth Tiger, Handicraft, Shanxi Province

Cloth Tiger, Handicraft, Shaanxi Province

Cloth Tiger, Handicraft, Shaanxi Province

Cloth Tiger, Handicraft, Henan Province

Cloth Tiger With Two Heads, Handicraft, Shaanxi Province

Cloth Tiger with a Fish Tail, Handicraft, Shanxi Province

c. Tiger Being Venerated as a Holy Guardian

As a gallant and powerful animal, the tiger has long been venerated as a guardian in China. Actually, it was as early as in the ancient time prior to Qin Dynasty (221BC—206BC) that the tiger had been widely taken as the gate god to dispel the evil spirits and protect the family. While in the Zhou Dynasty (1100BC—256BC), "tiger gate" was used to refer to the entrance to the royal palace, as what had been recorded in *Zhou Rites* and explained by Zheng Xuan, a famous scholar of Eastern Han Dynasty, to the effect that the gallantry of the tiger made it an ideal door keeper. Actually, the image of the tiger as a gate god was associated with the belief of the ancient Chinese that the animal devours ghosts. According to The *Book of Mountains and Seas*, all those ghosts that were proved evil by Shentu and Yulei, two great deities living with a giant peach tree on the holy Dushuo Moutain, would be bundled up and swallowed by the tiger. Therefore, people put the holy tiger together with Shentu, Yulei and the peach tree into a picture and pasted it on the door to dispel ghosts and evil spirits.

Tiger-head-shaped Hats, Handicraft, Passed on from Older Generations, Shaanxi Province

Tiger-head-shaped Gloves, Handicraft, Passed on from Older Generations

In Jin Dynasty, it was popular for many families to paint the tiger on the door on the eve of the Spring Festival, as what had been depicted in *Stories of Immortals* written by Gan Bao: "Towards the end of each year, it is a custom for people to draw a tiger on the door lit up by two lamps, which are assumed to be the eyes of the animal, to rid of misfortunes". While in the Tang Dynasty, it was believed that to draw the tiger-head on the door could cure one's illness, which had actually been recorded by Duan Chengshi in his book *Miscellaneous Morsels from Youyang*. At the present time, Chinese people still keep the custom in various ways. For example, the

Tiger-head-shaped Hats in Various Styles

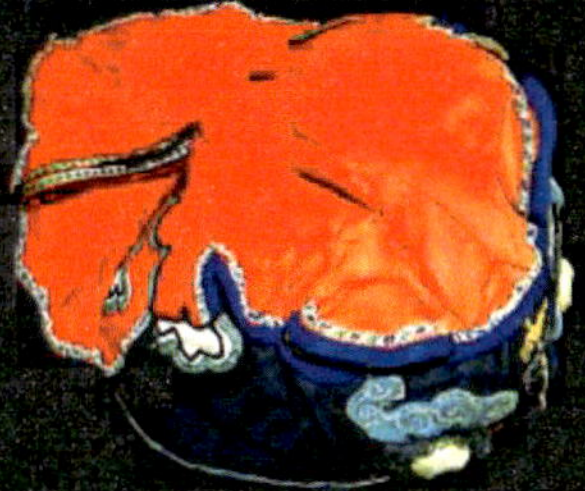

Tiger–head–shaped Hat

Tiger–head–shaped Hat Embroidered Through the Technique of Applique

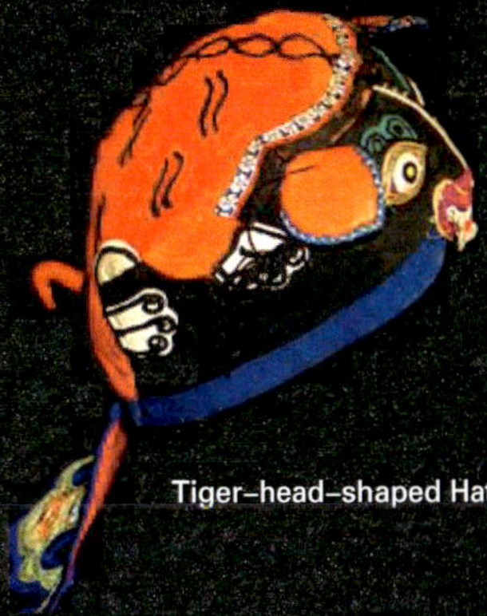

Tiger–head–shaped Hat

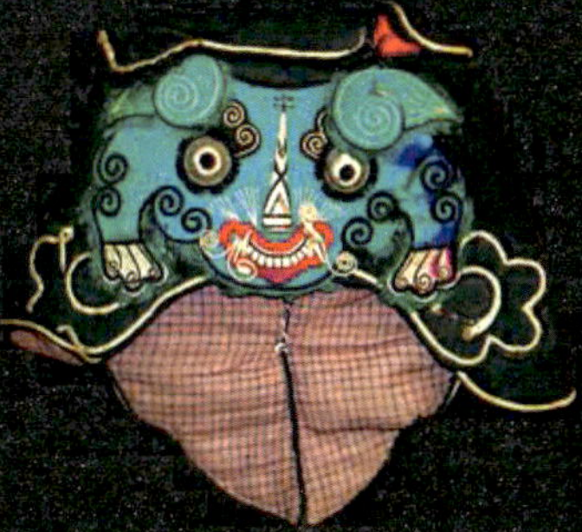

Tiger–head–shaped Hat

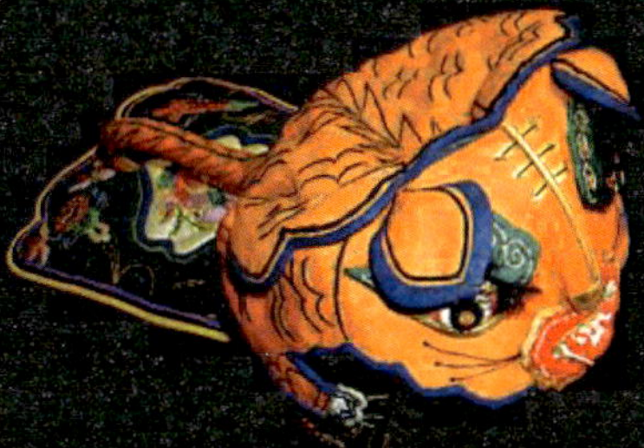

Tiger–head–shaped Hat with the Design Symbolizing Vigorous Re–productivity

Children's Hat with the Design Symbolizing a Promising Future

Longevity Hat for Children

Children's Hat with the Design of Deity Descending to the Land

Tiger–head–shaped Shoes

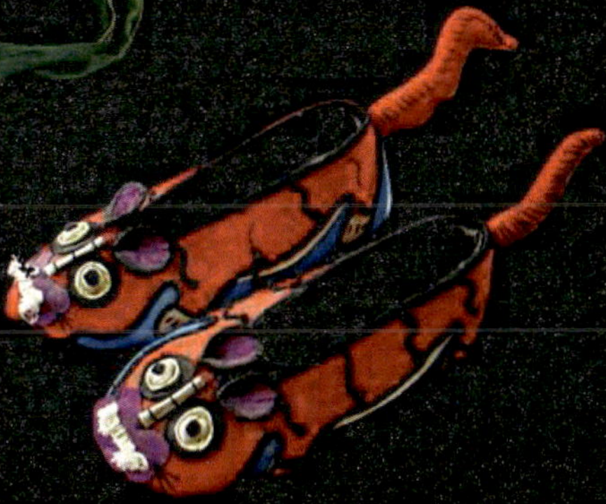

Tiger–head–shaped Shoes

Calamus Sword and the Gourd Carved with the Design of the Tiger, Qing Dynasty, Shandong Province

The Design of the Argyi-wormwood-made Tiger, Qing Dynasty, Shandong Province

The Taoist Master Riding the Argyi-wormwood-made Tiger, Paper Cut

Naxi people of Yunnan Province put up the painting “White Tiger, the Great Door-god” beside their entrance; the people of Weifang in Shandong Province would paste on the door the picture “Holy Tiger” on the Spring Festival; and in Zhangzhou of Fujian Province, the local citizens like to decorate their houses with the painting “Five Lucky Tigers” to celebrate the festival.

Actually, the tiger was regarded as a guardian not only for the living but also for the dead in ancient China as it was also taken as a holy animal to watch over tombs. Believing in animism, the ancient Chinese held that the tomb of the dead must be guarded as well. As the ruler of the animal kingdom, the tiger was naturally chosen as the ideal tomb keeper, which have been verified by recent archaeological discoveries. For example, the jade guardian unearthed from the ruins of the ancient Shang Dynasty was a tiger-headed statue indeed; the tomb-keeper of the Chu State in the Warring States Period which had been excavated at Xinyang, Henan Province was also a tiger-headed statue, with its mouth biting a wicked snake; likewise, many of the stone sculptures guarding the graveyard of Huo Qubing, a famous general of Western Han Dynasty, were shaped in the design of the tiger, which had been

Argyi-wormwood-made Tiger, Paper Cut, Shaanxi Province

Embroideries with the Design of the Tiger

Children's Overcoat with the Design of the Tiger Subduing the Five Pests, Passed on from Older Generations

Bellyband with the Design of the Tiger Subduing the Five Pests, Embroidery

Vest with the Design of the Five Pests Pieced Together in the Shape of Flowers, Gansu Province

Waistcoat with the Design of Repelling the Five Pests, Gansu Province

Pinafore with the Design of the Argyi–wormwood–made Tiger, Gansu Province

Jacket with the Design of Five Pests, Shanxi Province

delicately-carved and animatedly-moulded. In addition, the design of the tiger was also carved on coffins, stones and bricks in the tomb as a protector of the deceased in a symbolic sense in Han Dynasty. For hundreds of years, the tiger had been taken as a tomb guardian in China till Tang Dynasty, when the role was assumed by the lion.

The veneration of the tiger is also found in various Chinese customs, among which to give newly-born babies cloth-made tigers or tiger-shaped pillows as gifts is a popular one in the provinces of Shaanxi and Shanxi. When a baby is one month old, the uncle is expected to present the baby a gift of a yellow-cloth-made tiger with part of its tail being broken off and thrown away. By doing so, people extend the best wishes to the baby that it could grow up as strong as a tiger without being hurt by any disasters, which are believed to have been dispelled together with the broken tail of the tiger in a symbolic sense. To celebrate the birthday of a baby, the uncle would give the nephew or niece one or two tiger-shaped pillows as a present for it to sleep with or play with to express his beatitude. The mother, however, would usually make the so-called "tiger-headed shoes" or "tiger-headed cap" for the baby with the wish that the baby could grow up in good health and full vigour like a tiger.

As one of the most important celebrations in China, the Dragon Boat Festival also has lots of customs to venerate the tiger as a guardian. In addition to eating

Cutting off the Five Pests, Paper Cut, Beijing

Rooster Subduing the Five Pests, Paper Cut, Shanxi Province

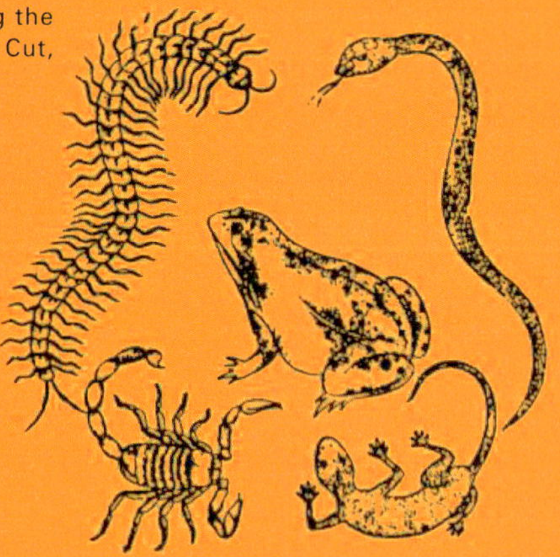

Picture of the Five Pests, from the *Selected Chinese Woodcut*

The Tiger Subduing the Five Pests, New Year Picture, Shanghai

The Tiger Trampling the Five Pests, Embroidery, Gansu Province

Lacquered Huzi, Hunan Province
It's a tiger-shaped lacquered chamber pot. Resembling the tiger, the pot has four legs crouching on the ground to support the body, with its tail bending upwards to the head to make the handle, and its head being raised to bulge out its open mouth.

Huzi, Bronze, Sixteen Kingdoms

Huzi, Celadon, West Jin Dynasty

White Glazed Porcelain Pillow with the Design of the Tiger on its Feet, Song Dynasty

Bronze Pillow with the Design of the Tiger Devouring the Bull, Warring States Period, Yunnan Province

glutinous rice dumplings, rowing dragon boats, hanging the argyi-wormwood-made tigers over the door is also very popular during the festival in many places. To hold the rite, people usually hang over the entrance a bundle of argyi wormwood, which would be originally tied up in the shape of a man and change into the form of a tiger gradually as a result of the air dry, with the purpose of scaring off the evil spirits. Actually, this interesting custom could date back to long time ago, which was recorded in details in *Festivals in the Jingchu Area* written by Liang Zonglin of the Southern Dynasties to the point that people would hang over the door a bundle of argyi wormwood tied up in the shape of a man to dispel calamities on May 5 every year. Down to the Qing Dynasty (1644—1911), Fucha Dunchong also depicted the convention in his *Yanjing Age in Mind*, "The Peking citizens would put a bundle of calamus or argyi wormwood beside the door to exorcise evils on the Dragon Boat Festival, which is an outgrowth of the tradition of hanging argyi-wormwood-made tiger over the door actually". Up to now, this tradition is still well kept in many places of China, including Beijing, where people would hang up over the door argyi-leaf-made tigers on the Dragon Boat Festival every year. In a similar sense, people in other places would cut the argyi wormwood or coloured paper into the shape of tigers, or paint tigers on the silkworm cocoon on May 5 each year to celebrate the festival.

Taking the tiger as a guardian is found in other customs of the Dragon Boat Festival as well. To avert misfortune, parents in North China would write the Chinese character " 王 " with the realgar wine on the forehead of the children on the festival, which is called the "tiger furrow". For the same purpose, children also wear perfume pouch made in the shape of tiger on that day. Likewise, little kids in such places as the provinces of Shandong, Zhejiang, Jiangsu, Fujian, mostly in the south, would wear on their back the so-called "Ai-tiger" for the festival, which is made of coloured silk cut into the shape of tigers and decorated with garlic, glutinous rice dumpling, the symbol representing the Chinese Eight Diagrams, etc. While in the Huaibei area of Anhui Province, children wear yellow-cloth-made bellyband and shoes on May 5 every year, upon which are embroidered the pattern of a tiger head together with the so-called "five pests" including the snake, the scorpion, the centipede, the gecko and the hornet, with the hope that the tiger would bring the poisonous pests under control. As part of the celebration for the Dragon Boat Festival, people living in the north-eastern part of Shandong Province including the counties of Penglai and Huangxian, would make silkworm-cocoon-tiger as a toy and a guardian for the children, which is made of silkworm cocoon filled with muddy pellet, with the two ends being moulded into the shape of the tiger-head.

Vase with the Design of Subduing the Dragon and Tiger, Porcelain, Qing Dynasty

Actually, the Chinese people venerate the tiger so much that they even take the animal as a protector of the male genitals, as revealed in the usage of the tiger-shaped chamber pot. The chamber pot, a widely used pottery among the people, was also nicknamed as "the little tiger", which was in fact based upon an ancient legend. It was said that General Li Guang, the famous archer of the Western Han Dynasty, once shot a tiger, whose bone was then made into a pillow for him to sleep with as a demonstration of his courage. What's more, to show his contempt towards the fierce animal, the general had his chamber pot made in the shape of the tiger. From then on, the vessel was given the nickname "the little tiger". In 1960, a chamber pot was unearthed from a tomb built in the West Jin Dynasty at Dantu, Jiangsu Province, which had been made exactly in the shape of a crouching tiger with delicately-moulded head, hair, legs and tail. According to the knowledge of folklore and cultural anthropology, the origin of the tiger-shaped chamber pot might be associated with the

Roaring Tiger, Porcelain

Dragon and Tiger, Brick Relief, Eastern Han Dynasty

symbolization of the animal. As what was recorded in *Baihu Tongyi*, a book about social culture written by Ying Shao of the Han Dynasty, the tiger, ruler of the animal kingdom, was such a masculine animal that it could not only defeat fierce animals but also bring the evil spirits under control. In addition, the eyesight of the animal is extraordinarily good at night with one of its eyes glittering and the other looking at things clearly. Therefore, it is easy to understand that the reason why the chamber pot is made in the shape of the tiger simply lies in the wish of people that the so-called "little tiger", as a guardian against devils, could protect the genitals from harm when one urinates. In the Chinese history, the tiger-shaped chamber pot had been used for centuries till it was prohibited in the Tang Dynasty because the grandfather of the Emperor Li Yuan was named after the tiger.

In addition, Chinese people also carve the design of the tiger on pottery pillows, hoping that the animal, as a powerful guardian, could protect them from the harm of evil spirits in their slumber.

d. Mutual Complement of the Tiger and the Dragon

As a symbol of vitality, the tiger is more often than not put side by side with the dragon in the traditional Chinese culture, either in complement or in opposition, to represent the animation of the Chinese nation in a symbolic sense. Since the tiger is the king on land, while the dragon the monarch in the sea, the union of the two

Stone *Qing* Carved with the Design of the Tiger, Shang Dynasty *Qing* is a kind of ancient percussion instrument of China.

Bronze *Ding*, Warring States Period, Anhui Province *Ding* is a kind of ancient cooking or ritual vessel of China.

Silver Clasp with the Design of a Winged Tiger, Western Han Dynasty, Yunnan Province

The Child Riding a Tiger, Dough Sculpture, Hebei Province

Pillow in the Shape of the Tiger-head and Fish-tail, Shaanxi Province

The Tiger Descending the Mountain, Paper Cut, Shaanxi Province

is regarded as a perfect alliance in the eyes of the Chinese people, which might be revealed in various aspects of the traditional Chinese culture. In the *Book of Changes*, one of the oldest masterpieces in Chinese philosophy, the dragon and tiger are taken to stand for heaven and earth, *yin* and *yang*, male and female respectively. While in the Chinese astronomy, the two imaginary beings are used to name different stars. In the similar sense, the dragon and the tiger are also employed in the field of strategics, medicine and calligraphy, as revealed in such related terms as "dragon/tiger tactic", "dragon and tiger acupuncture" and "dragon and tiger style". In addition, the two animals are utilized to designate calendars, bronze wares, festivals, national examination announcements in different periods of the Chinese history. Specially, the dragon and the tiger are regarded as the holy messengers that could guide one to the heaven, as what was described in the *Mirror Inscription on the Mountain Tai*, a book written in the Han Dynasty, that "Riding the dragon and guided by the white tiger, one could ascend to the heaven, enjoying the perpetual happiness of the immortal". According to the Chinese legend, the so-called Xiwangmu, ruler of the fairyland, usually rides the dragon and takes the tiger as her escort when she makes a tour. What is more, the dragon and tiger are also worshiped as the god of treasure by the Chinese people, which might be proved by the stone inscriptions of the Han Dynasty excavated in Shandong Province. As what has been mentioned in the introduction of the book, the tiger is very often associated with the dragon in many Chinese idioms, such as "covered talents like the hidden tiger and the crouching dragon", "dangerous spot as a dragon's pool and tiger's den", "a forbidding strategic point as one dominated by the tiger and the dragon". Obviously, the union of the tiger and the dragon has already become a symbol of mutual complement.

The union of the dragon and tiger is also found

Primary Member of the Court, Weifang New Year Picture Worshiped as the Mountain God by the people, the tiger dominates the animal kingdom. That accounts for why the primary member of the court is also compared to the tiger, as the title of the picture indicates.

in many cultural relics in China. In 1987, a pair of statues moulded out of mussels in the shapes of the dragon and the tiger respectively about 6,500 years ago, were excavated at Xishuipo, Anyang of Henan Province. In accordance with the traditional Chinese astronomic theory, the dragon was placed on the left of the dead in the tomb, while the tiger on the right. Actually, this rite reflected the Chinese people's religious beliefs at that time: on the one hand, the union of the two animals stood for the eternal reproduction of lives in that the dragon symbolized *yin* (literally the female gender) while tiger *yang* (literally the male gender); on the other hand, the two animals were assumed to have magic powers that could protect the dead from the harm of evil spirits. The two statues were so precious that they were hailed as "the first dragon" and "the first tiger" among the same kinds in China. In a similar sense, designs in the shape of the dragon and the tiger were found to be painted on the coffins unearthed from the

The Shadow Puppet of a Flying Tiger, Handicraft, Passed on from Old Generations, Gansu Province

Hilarity of the Tigers as an Auspice of the Spring, Painting, Shaanxi Province

Sculpture of the Tiger with Brown Glaze, Tang Dynasty, Hunan Province

Mawangdui tomb, in Changsha, Hunan Province, with the wish that the deceased could be blessed to ascend to the heaven.

It is believed that the cultural conception of the dragon-tiger union had been developed during the conflicts and integrations between different ethnic groups in the ancient Chinese history. According to historical research, the tiger used to be the totem of the tribes living in East China, while the dragon was worshiped among the people living in West China. In the remote antiquity, clashes and wars had probably

The Tiger Descending the Mountain, Carved Brick, Shanghai

Two Tigers Sharing One Head, Paper Cut, Shanxi Province

Facsimile of the Rock Painting of the Twelve Zodiac Animals, Inner Mongolia

broken out when the Qiang people, who were actually tiger-adoring nomads living originally in North-eastern China, immigrated to the central plain area of North China where the dragon-worshiping aborigines inhabited. As a result of the conflicts and communication among different ethnic groups, the Chinese people as a unified nation came into being. Meanwhile, the cultural conception of the tiger was also integrated into that of the dragon, as demonstrated in the designs carved on the bronze wares of the Shang Dynasty and Zhou Dynasty, which was usually made up of the imposing image of the tiger-head against the background with the picture of the dragon in the shadow.

Thereupon, the Chinese people venerated the dragon and tiger so much that they even took them to designate stars and directions. In order to gain spatial and temporal knowledge needed in their lives, the ancient nomads and farmers chose to study the operating rules of the sun, the moon and the stars, conceiving the constellations as certain images. As important totems, the dragon and tiger were thus taken to name stars by the ancient Chinese around 6,000 years ago. Taking the Big Dipper as an example, its handle is imagined as the head of the dragon, while its spoon the tail of the tiger, which could be compared in a symbolic sense to the above-mentioned statues shaped in the dragon and tiger respectively unearthed from the Mawangdui tomb. Among the so-called twenty-eight stars in the sky, the Chen star in the east is called the Dragon Star, which indicates the season of the spring; while the Shen star

The Tiger in Various Postures, Paper Cut

A Bronze Wine Vessel with the Design of the Tiger Devouring a Man, Shang Dynasty

Tiger and Bull Tray for Rituals, Bronze, Warring States Period, Yunnan Province

in the west is taken as the Tiger Star, which signifies the season of the autumn. For the ancient Chinese, one year was made of two seasons, namely the spring and the autumn, which were represented by the Dragon Star and the Tiger Star respectively. It was only later that the two seasons developed into four seasons along with a more complicated pattern of space-time. Towards the Spring and Autumn Period (770BC—476BC), the so-called dual celestial phenomena, as illustrated above, broke into four to symbolize the four directions in the space signified respectively by four holy animals, namely the dragon in the east, the tiger in the west, the peacock in the south, the tortoise in the north. The similar pattern of time was thus developed with the four seasons in the year symbolized by the imaginary animals above.

The ancient Chinese believed that the Dragon Star and the Tiger Star, among their same kinds, were the guardians for both the immortal Jade Emperor in the heaven and the human emperors on the earth. Therefore, the dragon and the tiger were often taken to symbolize emperors, as recorded in many Chinese historical books. According to the *Records of the Historian*, Liu Bang, the founding Emperor of the Han Dynasty, was once commented as "possessing the dragon-tiger air as what is specific to an emperor" before he won the throne, by Fan Zeng, an advisor to his rival Xiang Yu. Likewise, *History of the Southern Dynasties* also recorded that Emperor

Jade Tiger

Tiger Guards of the Door, Western Han Dynasty, Shaanxi Province

Jade Clasp Carved with the Design of the Dragon and Tiger A relic unearthed from the tomb of King of South Yue State

Wine Heater Carved with Four Holy Animals, Western Han Dynasty, Shaanxi Province Designed to heat up wine, the bronze ware was carved on its four sides with the so-called four holy animals, i.e. the blue dragon, the white tiger, the red bird and the black tortoise. In this picture, the white tiger was molded as a fierce and strong animal walking magnificently, with its tails bending upwards and Its mouth opening widely

Liangwu of the South Liang Dynasty was told once by an old man that he walked in such a dragon-tiger manner that he was destined to be the future emperor who would bring order to the chaotic nation as early as he was still a princelet.

Actually, the dragon and the tiger were regarded as not only the guardians of the Jade Emperor in the heaven and the human emperors on the earth, but also the patron saint of Taoism since they served as the protector when the Taoists made pills of immortality. While among the folks, the two animals were taken as affectionate guardians of the children too. For that reason, local people of Shaanxi Province, even at the present time, still give the newly-born baby tiger-headed, dragon-bodied and fish-tailed steamed breads as presents when it is one month old to wish the baby a good health and future.

However, the tiger was gradually overshadowed by the dragon in a long process, which had been somehow mystified and sanctified little by little in the Chinese history. Emperors tended to associate their throne with the dragon, calling themselves "Genuine Dragon, the son of the heaven", and claiming their offspring to be "the son or grandson of the Dragon". As a result, the handle of the royal seal, which had been dragon-tiger shaped in the Qin Dynasty, took the shape of the dragon solely in the Han Dynasty; without being accompanied by the tiger as before, the dragon alone was painted as the guardian on the royal lintels of the door in the Tang Dynasty; "dragon soaring" was used to indicate the throne-ascending of the emperor, while "tiger kowtowing" to show that ministers went down on their knees before the emperor. Nevertheless, both the tiger and the dragon were still regarded as propitious animals among the folks.

e. Taboos Concerning Tiger

As a ferocious animal, the tiger causes

Bronze Tiger Tally, Jin and South and North Dynasties

Pottery Tiger Glazed with Tri-colors, Tang Dynasty, Hunan Province

Tiger-shaped Container, Spring and Autumn Period

Tiger-shaped Stove Unearthed from the Tomb of Zhao Qing

Tiger-shaped Lacquer-work, Warring States Period

Tiger-head-shaped Pottery Nozzle, Warring States Period

Tiger-shaped Ornaments, Spring and Autumn Period or Warring States Period

a mixed feeling of adoration and fear in the heart of people. Naturally, the fear gives rise to lots of taboos among the folks. For example, the Chinese people used to put such things under taboo as giving birth to a baby in the tiger year, marrying a girl who was born in the tiger year, etc., because they believed that the tiger year was so ominous that those who were born in that year would be unfortunate or cold-hearted. Moreover, people born in the tiger year were also prohibited from paying a visit to the pregnant woman or the newly-born baby, or being engaged in the wedding night play.

Actually, the people of Miao living in Guizhou Province even go so far that the husband and wife would not sleep in the same bed on the tiger day of May every year for fear that they would be hurt by the animal, as what was described in the *Bamboo-leave Poems of the Miao People*, "Though looking at each other affectionately, the couple dare not sleep together since it is the tiger day of May".

Crouching Tigers, Clay Sculpture, Guizhou Province

Tigers and the Flying Twisted-Hair-Knot Baby, Paper Cut, Gansu Province

Tiger in Art Creation

Generally speaking, the tiger is a popular image frequently found in artistic works over different periods in the Chinese history. In the remote antiquity, a flock of tigers, as discovered later on, were drawn on the cliff in a valley (named after tiger) in Inner Mongolia, on which all the six tigers were portrayed in a vivid and distinctive manner in accordance with the aesthetic value of that time. Moreover, the design of the tiger, also carved on the rock but together with that of other eleven zodiac animals, was found in the heart of the Wulan Chabu Grassland of Inner Mongolia.

In the Shang Dynasty, the tiger was a popular design cast on bronze wares. For example, the dragon-tiger bronze statue unearthed from the Crescent River at Funan of Anhui Province in 1957, bore the bas-relief design of the tiger around its waist. While a drinking vessel excavated along the border of Anhua County and Ningxiang County in Hunan Province pictured incisively a horrific scene on its exterior, in which a tiger was devouring a human being.

Towards the end of the Shang Dynasty, the design of the tiger was also found in jade carving, as illustrated by a crouching jade tiger unearthed

The Design of the Chinese Character "寿" (Longevity) Encircled by Eight Tigers, Paper Cut, Shanxi Province

Tiger Glazed with Tri-colors, Jin Dynasty, Shanxi Province

Two Tigers, Clay Sculpture, Henan Province

The Tiger, Black Pottery, Shaanxi Province

Tiger-shaped Hanging Ornament, Modern, Shaanxi Province

Longevity Tiger, Paper Cut

Tiger-shaped Whistle, Song Dynasty, Liaoning Province

Tiger-shaped Doll, Clay Sculpture, Beijing

Crouching Tiger, Song Dynasty, Anhui Province

Porcelain Tigers, Qing Dynasty, Henan Province

The Tiger with a Straw Hat, Clay Sculpture, Henan Province

Big-headed Tiger, Clay Sculpture, Henan Province

from the No. 5 tomb of the ruin of the ancient Yin City at Anyang, Henan Province in 1976. The jade tiger was carved in such an artistic manner that the body of the animal was lengthened to a delicate lanky figure.

In the West Zhou Dynasty, many bronze wine vessels were also made in the shape of the tiger. Actually, a bronze vessel excavated in Baoji, Shaanxi Province was moulded into a masculine tiger that boasted a lengthy body, thick tail and strong legs.

Roaring Tigers, Clay Sculpture, Shaanxi Province

A bronze stand made in the Warring States Period have been unearthed in tomb No. 1 of the ancient Zhongshan State at Pingshan, Hebei Province. The stand was moulded into such a design that is made up of a tiger and a deer, with the former devouring the latter. What is impressive of the design is that the tiger was shaped into a very gallant animal with powerful legs, with a

Tiger-subduing Arhat, Painting, Porcelain

深山逢白额 努力搏腥风
父子俱无恙 脱离虎口中

Yang Xiang Fighting with the Tiger to Rescue His Father One of the paintings based on the Chinese Legend of the Twenty-four Filial Exemplars

mixed expression of nervousness and joyfulness radiated from its glaring eyes. While another copper stand made in the Western Han Dynasty, which had been excavated from the tomb of Liu Sheng in Mancheng of Hebei Province, was moulded into a crouching tiger, bearing the expression of solemn peacefulness on its face.

Tiger Tally began to be used in the army in the Warring States Period when warfare occurred most frequently. Issued to generals as imperial authorization for troop movement, the bronze or jade-made tally was shaped in the design of the tiger in halves, with one being held by the general and the other by the emperor. Only if the two inscription-bearing halves matched each other could the army be redeployed, which might be verified by both historical records and archaeological discoveries.

Moreover, the design of the tiger was also the component of architecture for both decoration and practical use in ancient China. For example, the pottery-made nozzle of drainpipes, which has been unearthed from the site of the ancient capital city of the Yan State at the Yi County, Hebei Province, was moulded in the shape of the tiger-head with simple but impressive designs. While in the Han Dynasty, graves were often guarded by crouching tigers made of stone, with the animal being carved on the brick and square wood of the tomb as well.

Specially, the image of the tiger also found expression in painting and calligraphy over the time in the Chinese history. Many calligraphers took great pleasure in writing the Chinese character " 虎 " ("hu", means tiger) with one stroke. Loved by people, young and old, the tiger was a popular image in paper-cutting; New Year's painting as well as toy-making at the same time.

Besides, the tiger is a lovely topic for children's songs. A very famous ballad that mocks the animal goes like this, "Two tigers are running, with great, great speed. It is really weird that one has no eyes below the forehead, while the other has no ears over the head!" Actually, early in the Song Dynasty, Su Shi, a famous poet of the time, also wrote in the style of children's songs about the animal metaphorically and humorously in his poem "*Staying-up for the Spring Festival*" on the very last evening of the tiger year, which reads to the effect that the tiger is to leave us for hunting, whose role to symbolize the year would be taken by the rabbit, dragon and snake, etc. one by one in the circle of twelve years so swiftly that no one could even stop it.

Tiger on Stamps

The first tiger-stamp was issued in Afghanistan in 1871. While the first New Year stamp in Japan was released in 1935. Due to World War II, the annual issue of the stamps had been stopped and was not resumed until the year 1948. Actually, it was to celebrate the coming tiger year of 1949 that the tiger-stamp was designed after the painting of "The Tiger" drawn by a Japanese artist.

In Taiwan of China, the annual issue of the stamp designed respectively in series after the image of the twelve zodiac animals representing one's year of birth was started in 1968. In due succession, the set of the dual tiger-stamps was issued in December 1973, both were designed after a tiger descending the mountain. The issue of the stamp of the twelve zodiac animals in the second series was made from the 1980 to 1991. The only difference of the stamp in the second series is that the images of the animals were in abstract forms, among which the dual tiger-stamps were no exception.

In Mainland China, the first series of the stamp of the twelve zodiac animals was issued from 1980 to 1991, in which one stamp makes one set. The second series was issued from 1992 to 2003, in which, however, one set includes two stamps, one being made in protruding pictures while the other in concave Chinese characters. In both series, the tiger stamps were designed with distinctive features.

Celebrities Born in the Year of the Tiger

It is a long tradition to associate a person's character and fate with the nature and traits of the animal he belongs to. Nowadays, some books about Chinese Zodiac Signs still take this characterization. However, seen from scientific perspective, the Chinese Zodiac Signs are no more than signs to record people's birth time. In the following part you will see a number of celebrities born under the Year of the Tiger. Both their merits and demerits have been recorded by historians, which testify to the fact that people born under the same animal year are not necessarily alike in personality and fate.

Qu Yuan

Qu Yuan (343BC.e—278BC.e), with Ping as his birth name, was a talented poet and loyal minister to the King of the State of Chu during the Warring States Period. As one of the most trusted ministers of the King, Qu was in charge of both internal and foreign affairs, advocating domestic reform and the foreign policy allying with the other states of the period against the hegemonic Qin state. Slandered by other jealous ministers, Qu was banished from the court by the King. Learning of the capture of his country's capital city in 278BC, he plunged into the Miluo River in today's Hunan Province, committing ritual suicide as a protest against the corruption of the politics. Being a master in verse, Qu was known for his more than twenty brilliant poetic works, among which "*Li Sao*" (*Grief of Parting*) and "*Tian Wen*" (*Questions about Heaven*) were the most famous pieces.

Qin Shihuang

Qin Shihuang (259BC—210BC), with Ying Zheng as his personal name, was the first emperor of China. As a thirteen-year-old boy, Ying Zheng succeeded the throne of the state of Qin, during the time of war with other states. At the age of twenty-two, he assumed the full power of the state, appointing worthy ministers to important positions. Thanks to his policy of befriending the distant states while attacking the nearby ones, Ying Zheng succeeded in subjugating the other six states one by one, thus unified China in 221BC. To celebrate this great achievement, Ying Zheng created a new title for himself known as the First Sovereign Qin Emperor, which was often shortened to Qin Shihuang. In order to consolidate the empire, Qin Shihuang not only standardized the system of law, coinage, metrology and the written language, but ordered to burn lots of books and suppressed scholars that were not to his liking. While to show off his power, the emperor made grand national tour of his empire for as many as five times. In order to fulfill the dream of being immortal, he ordered to search every corner of the nation for the elixir of life. For his after-life enjoyment, he built the magnificent Er Fang Palace and Li Shan Tomb at great expense of resources. Most important of all, to prevent the Xiongnu tribes from encroaching on the northern frontier, Qin Shihuang ordered the construction of an immense defensive wall known as the Great Wall, for the construction of which hundreds of thousands of men were mobilized, and an unknown number died... Good or evil, Qin Shihuang was the first powerful emperor in Chinese history.

Zhang Heng

Zhang Heng (78AD—139AD), with Pingzi as his courtesy name, was an astronomer and poet living in the Eastern Han Dynasty, who was known specially as the inventor of the celestial globe and the world's first seismometer. In memory of his great contributions to astronomy, an annular mountain on the moon discovered in 1970 was named after him; the No. 1802 minor planet of the solar system was also named in his honor in 1977. Moreover, Zhang, as a productive poet of his time, wrote lots of poems, among which "*Lyric Poems on Four Sorrows*", "*Western Metropolis Rhapsody*" and "*Eastern Metropolis Rhapsody*" were the most famous pieces.

Ruan Ji (210AD—263AD), was a man of letters and a thinker from the Kingdom of Wei (220AD—265AD) in the period of Three Kingdoms (220AD—280AD), with Colonel Ruan as his literary name since he used to serve in the army as a colonel of the infantry. Thanks to his literary contribution, Ruan, together with Ji Kang and other five worthy scholars of his time were hailed as the "Seven Sages of the Bamboo Grove" since they often gathered in the groves of bamboo to talk about literary issues. Being discontent with a gang of politicians in power in the court, Ruan Ji pretended to be insane and wandered everywhere to avoid persecution from his foes. The literary writing of Ruan includes such famous pieces as the self-expressive verse (*Yonghuaishi*) and the essay "*Biography of a Great Soul*".

Ruan Ji

Actually, in the Han Dynasty, both the Emperor Xuan, Liu Xun (91BC—49BC) and the important minister, Yang Zhen (54AD—124AD), were born in the Year of the Tiger. While in the period of Three Kingdoms (220AD—280AD), celebrities born in the Year of the Tiger also include Li Dian (174AD—209AD), a famous general, and Zhuge Jin (174AD—241AD), an important general, etc.

Yang Zhen

Gu Kaizhi (342AD—406AD), with "tiger head" as his infant name, was an outstanding artist in both painting and calligraphy in the East Jin Dynasty (317AD—420AD). Gu was well known for his talent in portrait painting, which is characterized by smooth lines and sharp edges. In addition, he was also gifted in calligraphy and the composition of poetry. Actually, Gu was so excellent that people believed few could rival him in terms of either intelligence, or talent in painting, or the indulgence in work. In summarizing painting theories, Gu wrote three books: namely, *On Painting*, *Introduction to Famous Paintings of Wei and Jin Dynasty* and *About the Painting of Yuntai Mountain.*

Other celebrities who were born in the Year of the Tiger in the Jin Dynasty include Du Yu (222AD—284AD), a military general and scholar, and Wang Rong (234AD—305AD), a personage in his time.

Yu Shinan (558AD—638AD), was a master in calligraphy in the early Tang Dynasty. Inheriting the merits of Wang Xizhi and Wang Xianzhi, two great artists in calligraphy of the Jin Dynasty, Yu developed his own style, which is characterized by outer flexibility but inner firmness. His authentic works that have been preserved till the present time include "Epitaph on Confucius Temple", "Inscription on the Tombstone of Princess Runan", and "Transcription of 'Preface to the Poems Composed at the Orchid Pavilion' by Wang Xizhi", among which the first two are his masterpieces.

Zhang Jiuling (678AD—740AD), with Zishou as his courtesy name, was a prominent minister, noted poet and established scholar of the Tang Dynasty, serving as the chancellor during the reign of Emperor Xuanzong. Zhang was such an upright and responsible minister in court that he had warned Emperor Xuanzong of the treason of An Lushan time and again, without fearing the possible persecution thus incurred. Due to the conspiracy organized by Li Linfu, a treacherous minister, he was removed from his position later on. Having made great contributions to the composition of the five-character poetry, Zhang was a celebrated poet of the Tang Dynasty at its peak. His writings had been collected in his 20-volume personal anthology *Collections of Zhang Qujiang*.

Zhang Jiuling

Gao Shi (702AD—765AD), with Dafu as his courtesy name, was a famous poet in the Tang Dynasty. As a veteran of the military service, Gao largely took the frontier life in the army as the subject matter in his seven-character poems, which not only depicted the impressive landscape, bloody battles of the west frontier, but also revealed the hardship of the soldiers and the delicate feelings of the local women, reflecting very well his patriotic heroism and persistent spirits. Gao Shi was a poet of somber realism, though romanticism was also a constant element of his poetic style. His representative work was a poem entitled "Nightlongings".

Other celebrities who were born in the Year of the Tiger in the Sui or Tang Dynasty also include Li Mi (582AD—618AD), leader of the Wagang Uprising towards the end of the Sui Dynasty (581AD—618AD), Pei Ji (570AD—632AD), prime minister in the early period of the Tang Dynasty (618AD—907AD) and Li Xian (654AD—684AD), prince of the Tang Dynasty whose posthumous title is "Zhang Huai", as well as the poet Li Qi (690AD—751AD), the celebrated premier Du Huangshang (738AD—808AD) and Emperor Xuan Zong (810AD—859AD)of the Tang Dynasty, whose personal name is Li Chen.

Hu Sansheng (1230—1302), with Shenzhi as his courtesy name, lived in the transitional period from the Song Dynasty to the Yuan Dynasty. He was the originator of the School of East Zhejiang Province in historiography. After the Song regime was overthrown by the Mongolian, Hu refused to take any position in the new government of the Yuan Dynasty. Instead, he spent half of his life in seclusion annotating *History as a Mirror*, the great classic in historiography, coming up with the book *Phonological Annotation of History as a Mirror*, through which he won himself a name in the field of historical studies.

Zhao Mengfu (1254—1322), with Zi-ang as his courtesy name and Songxue

Daoren as his pseudonym, was a celebrated painter, calligrapher and scholar in the Yuan Dynasty. Zhao made great achievements in many fields including poetry, calligraphy, painting and seal carving. Actually, he was so established in the art of calligraphy that the particular style he innovated was named after him as the "Zhao Style". In addition, the subject matter of his painting covered a great variety, ranging from landscape and human figure, birds and animals, to plants and flowers, which was almost unsurpassable for any artist of the later generation.

Zhao Mengfu

Other celebrities who were born in the Year of the Tiger in such dynasties as Liao, Song, Jin, Yuan and the so called Five Dynasties (907AD—960AD) also include the poet Du Xunhe (846AD—904AD) and the minister Feng Dao (882AD—954AD), the literateur Wang Yucheng (954—1001), the *Ci* writer Zhang Xian (990—1078), the poet Mei Yaochen (1002—1060), the expert in water conservancy Zheng Dan (1038—1103) and the famous general Liu Qi (1098—1162); together with Emperor Tian De (1122—1161) of the Jin Dynasty, whose personal name was Wuanyan Liang, and the historian of the Yuan Dynasty, Ma Duanlin (1254—1323), etc.

Yu Qian (1398—1457), whose courtesy name was Tingyi, was a famous strategist and statesman of the Ming Dynasty (1368—1644), with his outstanding achievements being recorded in the *History of the Ming Dynasty*. Yu's life was full of twists and turns. After Emperor Ying Zong was captured in the Tumubao Battle by a Mongolian tribe, he supported Zhu Qiyu as the new emperor and managed to safeguard the Capital City Beijing in the joint efforts with the army and the people. However, Yu was accused of treason and killed soon after the former emperor Ying Zong returned and took the throne again.

Tang Yin

Tang Yin (1470—1523), better known by his courtesy name Bohu, was an excellent painter, calligrapher and poet of the Ming Dynasty. His poems were fresh and natural, while his paintings were full of ease and innovation, in which both beautiful ladies and lofty mountains are depicted very often. Tang was hailed as the most gifted scholar of South China in the middle period of the Ming Dynasty .

Mei Yaochen

Gui Youguang (1506—1571) was an essayist of great fame in the Ming Dynasty, who was also known as Xifu by his courtesy name, and Zhengchuan or Xiangjisheng by his pseudonyms. Since he wrote mainly about the anecdotes of everyday life, his essays were fresh and natural to the reader. The most representative writings of him include "*A Brief Biography of My Mother*", "*Ode to the Burial of the Winter Flower*", "*Ode to My Study 'Xiang Jixuan'*", all of which were put in his personal collection *The Collected Writings of Zhengchuan*.

Li Shizhen (1518—1593), with Dongbi as his courtesy name, was a great master in the Chinese medicine of the Ming Dynasty, whose contribution to medicine was best demonstrated by his epic book *Bencao Gangmu* (*Compendium of Materia*

Li Shizhen

Medica) written in 13 years by traveling extensively across China, gaining first-hand experience with many herbs and local remedies.

Wang Shizhen (1526—1590), with Fumei as his courtesy name, was a famous man of letters and calligraphy critic in the Ming Dynasty. According to the historical record, Wang was an excellent critic of the art of calligraphy, though he himself was not good at writing. As for literary writing, Wang advocated that prose writers should imitate the style of the Pre-Han Dynasty while poets should follow that of the Tang Dynasty, for which he was regarded as the key member of the "Later Seven Masters" of the Old Phraseology Movement.

Wang Shizhen

Tang Xianzu (1550—1616), with Yireng as his courtesy name and Hairuoshi his alternative name, was known as "Shakespeare of China", whose masterpiece *Mudan Ting* (*Peony Pavilion*) was such a brilliant romantic drama that it was regarded as a milestone in the Chinese history of drama as well as in intellectual history as a whole.

Shi Kefa (1602—1645), was a respectable general of the Ming Dynasty, who earned his name in the resistance war against the advancing Manchu armies. Even after the Manchu army had taken a great proportion of the territory of the Ming Dynasty, Shi still dispatched his troops to fight against the invader with all his might. Besieged in the City of Yangzhou, he fought bravely with the Manchu army, refused to surrender and committed suicide after the city was taken. His writings were compiled in his personal collection *The Collected Writings of Shi Kefa*.

Shi Kefa

Other celebrities of the Ming Dynasty who were born in the Year of Tiger include: Song Lian (1310—1381), a man of letters; Wen Zhengming (1470—1559), an expert in painting and calligraphy; Li Kaixian (1502—1568), a famous dramatist; Qiu Ying (1506—1555), a painter; Liu Zongzhou (1578—1645), a thinker; Feng Menglong (1574—1646), a man of letters; Shen Defu (1578—1642), a litterateur; Qu Shisi (1590—1651), a famous minister in the court; Zhang Pu (1602—1641), a man of letters; Jin Junming (1602—1675), an expert in painting and calligraphy, etc.

Zhu Da (1626—1706), with Badashanren as his pseudonym, was the most famous painter and calligrapher during the transitional period from Ming Dynasty to Qing Dynasty. As a descendant of the Ming imperial line who had received classical education, Zhu was excellent in painting, calligraphy as well as poetry. In his painting, he adopted an abbreviated style to capture the very essence of the flowers and plants, and animals and other creatures he portrayed. In his calligraphy, which was somewhat the integration of that of Wang Xizhi, Yan Zhenqing and Wang Chong in style, Zhu deliberately used the bald-brush technique to show his dignity. His poetry, however, was full of strangeness, mystery and irony.

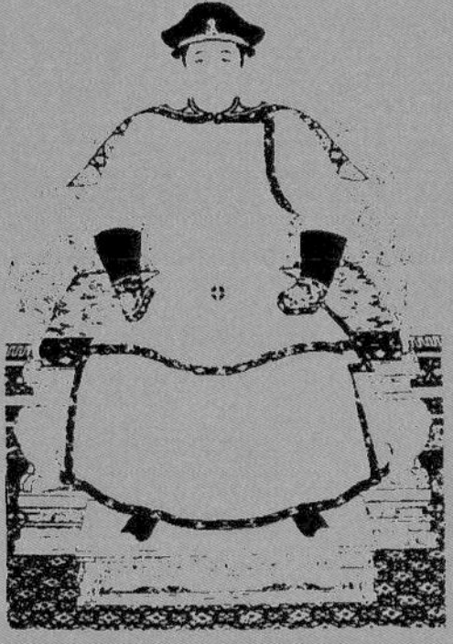

Emperor Shunzhi

Emperor Shunzhi (1638—1661), with Aixinjueluo Fulin as his personal name, was the third emperor of the Manchu-led Qing Dynasty, and officially the first Qing emperor to rule over China. As the ninth son of the Huang Taiji, who was also known as Emperor Taizong, Shunzhi ascended to the throne very young. The young emperor worked diligently and enthusiastically to make the country prosperous. To strengthen his rule, Shun Zhi had the *Great Qing Legal Code* enacted. Though he hoped to build a peaceful nation by allying the Manchu and Mongolian people with the Han people, the young emperor soon found that his efforts were in vain as the Manchu and Mongolian aristocracy stood in the way. Instigated by the eunuchs, Shunzhi was converted to Buddhism eventually. Having ruled the nation for 18 years, the emperor died in his youth.

Badashanren

Wan Sitong (1638—1702), with Jiye as his courtesy name, was a historian in the early Qing Dynasty. As a student of Huang Zongxi, the famous scholar in the late Ming Dynasty, Wan was known as a key member of the School of the East Zhejiang Province, a celebrated association for historical studies. In spite of the fame as a scholar specialized in historiography, especially in the history of the Ming Dynasty, he refused to undertake any official position in the Qing court. However, Wan contributed to the compiling of the *History of the Ming Dynasty* on condition that he received no title nor salary from the Qing government for as long as 19 years till the draft of the book was completed.

Emperor Daoguang

Wang Mingsheng (1722—1797), with Feng Jie as his courtesy name, was a historian and expert in the study of Confucian classics in Qing Dynasty. He adopted empirical methodology in his research, which covers such issues as the political system, historical figures, tablet inscription, geographical discovery, etc. In order to probe into the laws, regulations and historical events in ancient China, Wang wrote the book *Discussions on the Seventeen Dynasties*, which established his fame as an important scholar of historiography in the Chinese history.

Emperor Daoguang (1782—1850), with Aixinjueluo Minning as his personal name, was the first emperor in the 2000-year history of the Chinese monarchy who signed an unfair treaty with the western powers to surrender China's sovereignty rights under humiliating terms. Inheriting the throne in his middle age, Daoguang had once endeavored to revive the old dynasty by taking active measures, among which the most well-known one is to appoint Lin Zexu as the commissioner to ban the opium trade in Guangdong Province. However, due to the decline of the empire, he finally failed in the First Opium War with Britain.

Wei Yuan (1794—1857), with Moshen as his courtesy name, was a historian, thinker and man of letters in modern China. Living in the declining Qing Dynasty when it was ruled by Emperor Jiaqing and then by Emperor Daoguang, Wei Yuan was deeply concerned with the crisis facing China at that time. As a patriotic scholar, he advocated learning the advanced science and technology from the west to resist against the foreign invasion. Wei was best known for his monumental work *Illustrated Treatise on the Maritime Kingdoms*, in which he put forward his famous political proposal of "resisting the foreigners with the technology learned from them".

Weng Tonghe (1830—1904), with Shengfu as his courtesy name, was an influential statesman and calligrapher in the modern time of China, who was especially known as the imperial tutor of Emperor Tongzhi and Emperor Guangxu. Weng was a hawk in the court, advocating fighting against the enemy in both the Sino-Japanese war in 1894 and the war with France from 1883 to 1885. At the same time, he was a reformist, proposing a radical reform of the administration of the government in opposition to the conservative "westernization group" headed by Li Hongzhang. As a calligrapher, Weng had integrated the merits of other artists into his own, evolving his particular vigorous and forceful style.

Weng Tonghe

Shi Dakai (1830—1863) was an outstanding military leader of the Heavenly Kingdom of Great Peace (1851—1864) established by Hong Xiuquan in the uprising against Qing Dynasty. As an important figure of the uprising, Shi was in charge of the military affairs, bringing about lots of victories to the newly-built Kingdom. Nevertheless, distrusted by Hong Xiuquan, he was forced to leave to fight separately against Qing troops in South China with the men loyal to him. Besieged by the Dadu River in Sichuan Province, he was forced to surrender in order to save his army and was eventually executed by Qing troops.

Wang Xianqian (1842—1917), with Yiwu as his courtesy name and Kuiyuan as his pseudonym, was a master of the classical Chinese learning and the last director of the Yuelu Academy, an institute for the classical scholarship in China. Reading extensively, Wang was an extremely knowledgeable while modest scholar. At the same time, he was serious and strict in his empirical research, at which he was so good that he made great achievements in many fields including historiography, literary study, studies of the Confucian classics, etc. Moreover, Wang was also known as a specialist in the research of ancient books in that he had written, compiled, annotated or revised more than 50 volumes of classics.

Yan Fu (1854—1921), with Youling as his courtesy name, was a translator and pioneering thinker towards the end of Qing Dynasty. When sent to Britain to learn naval technology, Yan soon became

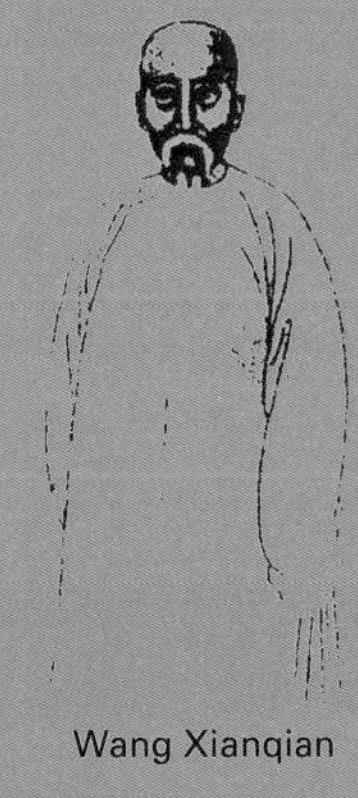
Wang Xianqian

interested in the western natural sciences and social and political theories. Having returned to China, he systematically translated into Chinese many western works in social and political studies, among which *Tianyanlun*, the Chinese translation of T. H. Huxley's essay "Evolution and Ethics" was the best known in China. Moreover, he proposed the abolishment of stereotyped writing styles and the establishment of modern schools to reform the education system of China. As a scholar of profound idea and knowledge, Yan Fu had exerted great influence on both the intelligentsia and the education system of modern China.

Yan Fu

Sun Yat-sen

Sun Yat-sen (1866—1925), with Wen as his birth name and Yat-sen as his courtesy name, was the great pioneer in the democratic revolution towards the end of Qing Dynasty. Though originally trained as a doctor, Sun gave up his medical practice later for his political career to found the Society for Reviving China, which was developed into the famous United League of China in joint efforts with other revolutionary organizations. Elected as the premier of the United League, Sun put forward the "Three Principles of the People" that concerns about the sovereignty of the nation, the civil rights of the people and the livelihood of the people respectively so as to bring an end to the rule of Qing Dynasty and the domination of the imperialists, to equalize the ownership of land, to found a republic for the people and eventually to bring a revival to China. In addition, he also started a newspaper to publicize his revolutionary principles. After the 1911 revolution, Sun was elected the provisional president of China. However, he was forced to resign due to the concession of other revolutionists in 1912 and went back to office in 1921 as the president proper. Having defeated the rebellious troops headed by Chen Jiongming, Sun Yat-sen was determined to reorganize the National Party. Under his leadership, the first national congress of the party was held in January 1924. On the congress, the proclamation of the reorganization of the National Party was announced, which set down the policy of allying with the Soviet Union and the Chinese Communist Party, and assisting the farmer and worker at the same time.

Other celebrities of Qing Dynasty who were born in the Year of the Tiger include: Zha Shenxing (1650—1727), a poet; Tian Wenjing (1662—1732), governor of Hedong; Li Wei (1686—1738), governor of Zhili Province; Liu Dakui (1698—1779), an essayist; Hong Liangji (1746—1809), an expert in the study of Confucius classics; Mu Zhang'a (1782—1856), a royal scholar; Ding Yan (1794—1876), an educator; Zheng Zhen (1804—1864), another educator; Xu Shou (1818—1884), a pioneer scientist in Chemistry in modern China; Duolong'a (1818—1864), a general of the Manchu army who had suppressed the Taiping Uprising; Feng Zicai (1818—1903), a famous patriotic general; Li Ciming (1830—1894), a man of letters; Liu Kunyi (1830—1902), an industrialist in the westernization movement in late Qing Dynasty; Zheng Guanying (1842—1922),a pioneer thinker in modern times; Wu Tingfang (1842—1922), a jurist and diplomat in modern China; Luo Zhenyu (1866—1940), a scholar in modern times, etc.

虎